access to history

The CHANGING NATURE *of* WARFARE 1700–1945

access to history

themes

The CHANGING NATURE *of* WARFARE 1700–1945

Neil Stewart

HODDER
EDUCATION
AN HACHETTE UK COMPANY

Acknowledgements

The front cover shows 'La Mitrailleuse' (1915) by C. R. W. Nevinson, Tate Gallery.

The publishers would like to thank the following individuals, institutions and companies for permission to reproduce copyright illustrations in this book:
Bildarchive Preussischer Kulturbesitz, page 79; British Museum, pages 37, 41 (bottom), 49; Corbis, pages 115, 132; Hulton Getty, page 87; Hulton Archive, page 63; Illustrated London News Picture Library, page 65; Mansell/TimePix/Rex Features, page 41 (top); National Army Museum page 9; *Punch*, page 95; The National Library of Wales, page 122.

Every effort has been made to trace and acknowledge ownership of copyright. The publishers will be glad to make suitable arrangements with any copyright holders whom it has not been able to contact.

Orders: please contact Bookpoint Ltd, 130 Milton Park, Abingdon, Oxon OX14 4SB. Telephone (44) 01235 827720 Fax: (44) 01235 400454. Lines are open from 9.00am-5.00pm, Monday to Saturday, with a 24 hour message answering service. You can also order through our website www.hoddereducation.co.uk

British Library Cataloguing in Publication Data
A Catalogue record for this title is available from the British Library

ISBN-13: 978 0 340 78075 6

First published 2001
Impression number 14
Year   2015

Copyright © 2001 Neil Stewart

Typeset by Fakenham Photosetting Limited, Fakenham, Norfolk.
Printed in Great Britain for Hodder Education, an Hachette UK Company, Carmelite House, 50 Victoria Embankment, London EC4Y 0DZ by CPI Group (UK) Ltd, Croydon, CR0 4YY

Contents

Preface

The original *Access to History* series was conceived as a collection of sets of books covering popular chronological periods in British history, together with the histories of other countries, such as France, Germany, Russia and the USA. This arrangement complemented the way in which history has traditionally been taught in sixth forms, colleges and universities. In recent years, however, other ways of dividing up the past have become increasingly popular. In particular, there has been a greater emphasis on studying relatively brief periods in considerable detail and on comparing similar historical phenomena in different countries. These developments have generated a demand for appropriate learning materials, and, in response, two new 'strands' have been added to the main series – *In Depth* and *Themes*. The new volumes build directly on the features that have made *Access to History* so popular.

To the general reader

Access books have been specifically designed to meet the needs of examination students, but they also have much to offer the general reader. The authors are committed to the belief that good history must not only be accurate, up-to-date and scholarly, but also clearly and attractively written. The main body of the text (excluding the Study Guide sections) should therefore form a readable and engaging survey of a topic. Moreover, each author has aimed not merely to provide as clear an explanation as possible of what happened in the past but also to stimulate readers and to challenge them into thinking for themselves about the past and its significance. Thus, although no prior knowledge is expected from the reader, he or she is treated as an intelligent and thinking person throughout. The author tends to share ideas and explore possibilities, instead of delivering so-called 'historical truths' from on high.

To the student reader

It is intended that *Access* books should be used by students studying history at a higher level. Its volumes are all designed to be working texts, which should be reasonably clear on a first reading but which will benefit from re-reading and close study.

To be an effective and successful student, you need to budget your time wisely. Hence you should think carefully about how important the material in a particular book is for you. If you simply need to acquire a general grasp of a topic, the following approach will probably be effective:

1. Read Chapter 1, which should give you an overview of the whole book, and think about its contents.

2. Skim through Chapter 2, paying particular attention to the 'Points to Consider' box and to the 'Key Issue' highlighted at the start of each section. Decide if you need to read the whole chapter.
3. If you do, read the chapter, stopping at the end of every sub-division of the text to make notes.
4. Repeat stage 2 (and stage 3 where appropriate) for the other chapters.

If, however, your course demands a detailed knowledge of the contents of the book, you will need to be correspondingly more thorough. There is no perfect way of studying, and it is particularly worthwhile experimenting with different styles of note-making to find the one that best suits you. Nevertheless the following plan of action is worth trying:

1. Read a whole chapter quickly, preferably at one sitting. Avoid the temptation – which may be very great – to make notes at this stage.
2. Study the diagram at the end of the chapter, ensuring that you understand the general 'shape' of what you have read.
3. Re-read the chapter more slowly, this time taking notes. You may well be amazed at how much more intelligible and straightforward the material seems on a second reading – and your notes will be correspondingly more useful to you when you have to write an essay or revise for an exam. In the long run, reading a chapter twice can, in fact, often save time. Be sure to make your notes in a clear, orderly fashion, and spread them out so that, if necessary, you can later add extra information.
4. The Study Guide sections will be particularly valuable for those taking AS Level, A Level and Higher. Read the advice on essay questions, and do tackle the specimen titles. (Remember that if learning is to be effective, it must be active. No one – alas – has yet devised any substitute for real effort. It is up to you to make up your own mind on the key issues in any topic.)
5. Attempt the source-based questions section. The guidance on tackling these exercises is well worth reading and thinking about.

When you have finished the main chapters, go through the 'Further Reading' section. Remember that no single book can ever do more than introduce a topic, and it is to be hoped that, time permitting, you will want to read more widely. If *Access* books help you to discover just how diverse and fascinating the human past can be, the series will have succeeded in its aim – and you will experience that enthusiasm for the subject which, along with efficient learning, is the hallmark of the best students.

Robert Pearce

Introduction: The Nature of Warfare

POINTS TO CONSIDER

This chapter introduces you to the scope of the book, the periods covered and the features of warfare. The significant features of war are explained, allowing you to explore their impact in each of the succeeding chapters.

1 The Scope of the Study

KEY ISSUE What have been some of the influences of warfare on European society?

War has been one of the most direct and major influences on human history. It has determined the shape and size of our countries and made possible great empires. It has been a driving force behind technological innovation and it has shaped our societies and our cultural values. War has even determined the languages we speak: the language of the conqueror follows his armies. Just as war has shaped society, so the nature of warfare has been determined by the society in which it arose. Warfare cannot be isolated from the environment in which it occurs, and so war must be studied in its political, economic, social and cultural framework.

This book traces the inter-relationship between society and the conduct of war from 1700 to 1945. The chapters that follow concentrate on those periods that represent distinct steps in the evolution towards modern warfare. Our starting point is a survey of the nature of warfare in the eighteenth century, the age of dynastic armies fighting limited wars for their kings. This is followed by the challenge to the kings and their armies represented by the French Revolution and Napoleon. The study then examines the next major influence on the conduct of war, the impact of industrialisation. The two World Wars are examined in depth due to their transforming effect on the nature of warfare. The final chapter offers some pointers on post-1945 developments and future war as well as conclusions drawn from across the whole period.

A book that sets itself such an extended time span cannot attempt to cover all campaigns, nor to provide a chronological account of the course of wars. Geographically the book confines itself mainly to events in Europe, though the United States has also been drawn into the analysis due to its significant participation in the two World Wars.

There is also an attempt to concentrate primarily on land warfare, although by necessity this must include the contribution of air power.

2 The Features of Warfare

> **KEY ISSUE** What are the major features of warfare?

The focus of this study is on the consistent features of war in each of the periods covered. These include resources, technology, leadership, tactics and strategy, organisation and logistics, the composition of armed forces, and public opinion, morale and propaganda. Although these features are presented separately in the context of their period, they should not be seen in isolation. At certain times and in certain circumstances some of these features will be more significant than others. But in all periods the nature of warfare, armies and their relationship to society are shaped by the inter-relationship of all of these features.

a) Economic Factors

One of the major features of war in all periods is the material wealth of the war-maker. Although this may be calculated in different ways in different periods, it remains one of the most basic elements in the waging of war. War is the most expensive activity a country can undertake. The wealth and resources of the war-makers determine the size of their armies, and how long they can be maintained and equipped. The cost of war is often decisive in determining the length of a war; if no strategic breakthroughs are made then war continues until one side collapses economically before the other. Commanders and politicians have placed economic warfare at the heart of their strategies. From the time of the French Revolution, the protection and maximisation of one's own resources and the disruption of the enemy's economy and supplies has been vital. It has played a major part in deciding the outcome of the Napoleonic wars, the two World Wars and even the Cold War.

b) Technology

Another perennial feature of warfare that must be taken into account is the prevailing state of technology in both the military and non-military fields. Throughout history great emphasis has been placed on gaining and developing the most effective weapons, those that have greater range, accuracy and firepower – those that are more deadly! The type of weapons available is the major determinant of strategy and tactics and shapes the nature of wars. For example, the type of weapons available to armies on the Western Front in the First World

War gave the advantage to the defenders and produced a stalemate of defensive trenches. But by the Second World War the technology of weapons had moved on allowing for a more mobile war which favoured the attacker. Yet we must be cautious in this respect: technology only creates possibilities. The fact that a weapon has been invented does not mean to say that it would be taken up or used in the most appropriate fashion. The invention of the machine gun and the tank are examples of powerful new weapons initially not being used effectively due to cultural resistance, cost or a misunderstanding of their full potential. One consistent rule of military technology is that with every generation that passes new weapons are developed or older ones are improved, making them more destructive. Each new major war therefore has the potential to cause more deaths than the one before.

Just as important as innovations in weapons technology were developments in non-military technology that could be adapted for the war effort. These developments were largely in transport, communications and detection and, although they were not designed for military purposes, they often had a revolutionary impact on the nature of warfare. In the nineteenth century the scale of war was expanded by the steam engine. At sea this was applied to the steamboat, transforming trans-oceanic warfare and helping establish worldwide European empires. On land it led to rail transport which radically altered the conduct of war. Railways were able to transport whole armies and their supplies to the battlefield in a fraction of the time taken previously. The greatest impact of the railways was on the size of armies, as they shattered the constraints of horse-drawn supplies. With the adoption of railways to warfare millions of men could be delivered to the battlefield within days. In the twentieth century the development of the internal combustion engine and the aeroplane had an equally revolutionary impact. In the field of communications, the military use of the telegraph, radio and the telephone had a dramatic effect on the operational control and co-ordination of military actions. As the twentieth century wore on, the military application of radar, nuclear power and the computer once again reshaped the conduct of war.

c) Leadership

Perhaps the most high-profile element of war is leadership. Examples of leaders in war are provided in the following chapters, with an analysis of their strengths and weaknesses. The leaders profiled are: Frederick the Great, Napoleon, Ludendorff, Haig, Churchill, Hitler, Stalin and Roosevelt. Some of these figures are solely military commanders, the majority are political leaders who, for good or ill, also acted as military leaders. The impact of leadership in war is often elevated above other characteristics of warfare, as conflicts can more easily and dramatically be portrayed as personal struggles between rival leaders. There is a greater public fascination in the gladiatorial battle between great men than there is over the intricacies of technology or the detail of logistics. Certainly the character and ambition of men like Frederick the Great, Napoleon and Hitler had a major effect on the conflicts in which they were involved, but they were not the only factor in determining the outcome of their wars. We must keep in mind the fact that a leader's personal contribution is only one element in a series of interlocking features of warfare.

d) Tactics, Strategy and Doctrine

A feature of war often closely associated with leadership concerns the purpose and direction of forces in war. This can be seen at two levels. At the higher level, the defined aims and conduct of the war effort are referred to as strategy. This sets the basic aim of the campaign and general guidance on how it may be achieved. The method by which these aims are secured is referred to as tactics. Strategy is determined by the political and/or the military leaders; tactics on the ground are usually the responsibility of the military leaders, often devolved down to the troops in the field. To provide an analogy from the business world, in an office the boss sets the strategy, while the secretary handles the tactics.

The relationship between strategy and tactics is crucial: they must be in harmony or disaster will ensue. The German forces in the Second World War displayed brilliant tactical effectiveness throughout the conflict, but they were handicapped by Hitler's strategy that became increasingly misjudged, chaotic and driven by racist hatreds. In the earlier periods Frederick the Great and Napoleon personally led their forces and set both strategy and tactics. In the later periods, with the great expansion of armies and the scale of their operations, commanders or political leaders could set strategy but they could not be in place to decide tactics. The more flexible and effective armies, such as the German army, made a virtue of delegating tactical responsibility down to the most junior level.

Above tactics and strategy is the doctrine of war. This is the overarching concept of how a nation's forces will approach war. It can arise from a number of sources: the prevailing military theories, the views of the dominant military/political leader or a nation's recent experience. For example, in their preparations for the Second World War the French army, after having been traumatised by their experience and losses of the First World War, had an established doctrine of defensive war. Unfortunately technology and tactics had moved on since 1918, giving the advantage to the attacking forces. The result was the defeat of France in six weeks.

e) Supplies

Probably the least glamorous feature of war is what is now referred to as logistics. This involves the procurement and delivery of supplies (food, fodder for horses, arms and equipment) and personnel. The effective provision of these supplies has won as many battles as inspired leadership. Indeed the mark of a good leader was often measured by how well he could keep his forces supplied on campaign. Marlborough's tremendous logistical feat in organising supplies for his army in their dramatic 250 mile march from the Netherlands to the Danube to secure his victory at Blenheim in 1704 was considered one of the wonders of the age. Just as the guaranteed provision of supplies could win campaigns, so the lack of those materials could destroy a campaign and with it the entire war effort, as both Napoleon and Hitler discovered in their badly prepared and poorly supplied invasions of Russia.

f) Public Opinion

Another feature of warfare that has increasing significance as the period under study progresses is the role of public opinion. At the beginning of the study, in the eighteenth century, the only opinion that a king valued was that of his fellow kings. In an age before mass literacy or modern democracy few channels existed for the expression of opinion. If discontent did surface, the king's army crushed it. The ideological challenge of the French Revolution and the increased size of armies in the Revolutionary and Napoleonic Wars demanded the support and mobilisation of the nation. Domestic public opinion had to be shaped for the conflict and, if possible, the enemy's morale deflated. This process grew steadily through the nineteenth century with the expansion of the franchise, literacy rates and the popular press. It reached its peak with the total war effort required in the two World Wars of the twentieth century, and has continuing importance in the post-1945 period.

The next chapter provides a survey of the major features of war in the context of the eighteenth century and establishes a framework against which later changes can be compared.

Summary Diagram
The Nature of Warfare

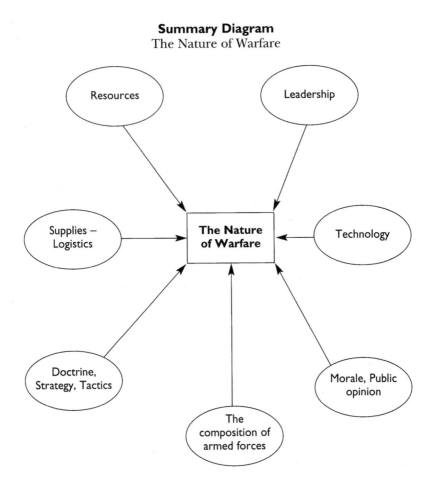

Dynastic Warfare 1700–1789

POINTS TO CONSIDER

This chapter provides you with the basic elements of warfare in the eighteenth century and acts as a framework against which you can compare the same elements in later periods. The major features highlighted include the type of men in the army, their training, the weapons, tactics and experience of war, and the problems of supply. There is also an assessment of the importance of leadership using Frederick the Great as a case study.

KEY DATES

1690–1710	Introduction of the bayonet and the flintlock musket which increases firepower and changes battlefield tactics.
1701–1714	The War of the Spanish Succession: Britain, Austria and the Netherlands prevent the union of France and Spain.
1740	Frederick II becomes King of Prussia, seizes Silesia from Austria.
1756–63	The Seven Years War. Prussia emerges as a great power.
1760–1780s	Technical advances in artillery produces lighter, more manoeuvrable cannons.
1789	Beginning of the French Revolution

1 The Emergence of Professional Armies

> **KEY ISSUE** What were the reasons for the emergence of professional armies?

From the end of the Middle Ages to the American and French Revolutions, armies were the possessions not of nations but of dynasties, the royal families. These armies were used to settle disputes with rivals, to win colonies and to keep their sovereigns in power. By the eighteenth century armies were increasingly professional and effective and placed undreamt of power in the hands of their monarchs. So vital to a king's wealth and security were they that dynastic states reorganised themselves to fund the most powerful force they could possibly afford.

By 1700 we can see the gradual emergence of professional armies across Europe. The officers and men were less likely to be mercenaries moving from one army to another and were now permanent, and paid, servants of their sovereign. The armies were increasingly full-time or 'standing' armies, which the king had to pay, feed, arm, clothe and house in both war and peace. This represented a massive change to the size and nature of armies and imposed vastly increased costs on their royal masters, but it was a cost worth paying. An effective professional army was able to guarantee security from abroad and perhaps win territories or trading rights. This in itself brought greater stability at home; but, more than this, armies were used internally to put down rebellions, thus strengthening the King's control on his realm. Monarchs were ensuring that they alone had a monopoly of force in their societies. With greater control a king was able to enforce a massively increased tax yield, most of which would be spent on the armed forces. The consequences of this process were immense as the size of armies and the power of the dynastic states grew dramatically.

2 The Men at Arms

> **KEY ISSUE** What types of men were drawn into the armed forces?

a) Officers and Lower Ranks

The social make-up of the King's forces was an exaggerated reflection of eighteenth-century civilian society. Generally, more than nine out of ten commissioned officers were drawn from the nobility: the higher their aristocratic status, the higher their rank. Officer commissions were purchased, providing a useful contribution to state funds, but overwhelmingly by wealthy aristocrats. The British army was the most commercialised in this respect, with every rank having a price upon it. They were bought and sold as if they were a piece of property or a business, which in effect many of them were. It was still possible for aristocratic officers, who saw themselves as an international elite, to move from one sovereign's employment to another's without arousing any ill will. However, it became increasingly more practical to make use of home-based aristocrats with their ready supply of conscripts from their own estates and their stronger bonds of loyalty and obedience to their monarch.

At the other end of the social scale, those men who were conscripted or forced into the armies were not a true reflection of the lower orders of society, especially in Western Europe. Here prosperity grew in the wake of a more ordered society and provided greater employment opportunities. With the removal of the greatest recruiting agent, hunger, it became increasingly difficult to meet the manpower requirements of the expanded armies. It was clearly recognised that the most productive members of the workforce were more useful to the economy by remaining at work in their estates or towns to pay for the wars, not to fight in them. This only left the less useful members of society for the armies to draw upon. As Michael Howard says, 'it became more difficult to recruit into the ranks of the armies

William Bunbury, 'Recruits', c. 1780. The sick, the destitute and the feeble-minded are 'recruited' directly from the alehouse, to the derision of onlookers.

anyone except social drop-outs, criminals, dupes and half-wits who could only be kept under control by ferocious discipline.'[1]

b) Recruitment

The increased demand for manpower in the expanding armies meant that recruitment remained a problem throughout the century, but it was during wartime, when armies had to be raised quickly and losses were high, that the greatest difficulties arose. It was common for prisons to be emptied directly into the army; unlucky civilians, often from abroad, were seized by force ('press-ganged'); and prisoners of war were seen as valuable replacement troops. The problem was made more difficult by the enormous loss of troops through disease and desertion rather than death in battle. In wars up to the mid-nineteenth century, losses due to sickness in armies outnumbered death in action in the proportion of five to one (in the twentieth century the opposite was the case). During the Seven Years War (1756–63) the French lost as much as a fifth of their army each year due to disease, desertion and battle, requiring 50,000 replacements annually. During the same war Prussia lost as many as 80,000 men by desertion alone. Desertion was so widespread that it directly influenced and constrained tactics and logistics. Prussian commanders were ordered to avoid camping or fighting in forested or hilly areas that provided opportunity for escape. Night marches, foraging, open pursuit of the enemy, and advance patrols were strictly controlled or simply prohibited. The Prussian figures, however, were dwarfed by the losses to the huge Russian army from all causes leading to an estimated 50 per cent replacement every year

It was ruinously expensive to keep a large standing army in peacetime, but it was dangerous to be caught unprepared at the outbreak of war. One method of raising troops quickly in time of war was through a reserve militia drawn from an aristocrat's estates, trained by him (outside the growing season) and called into the army when required. The Russians and the Prussians were the most advanced in this respect and effectively militarised their agrarian societies. Another important and substantial source of men in time of war was from abroad. This was not a sign of weakness but a rational deployment of the king's resources. To hire men from abroad allowed a monarch to retain his most efficient workforce on the land and avoided their destruction in battle. Throughout the eighteenth century half of both Prussia's and Britain's forces were composed of foreign troops. Some countries specialised in the hiring out of their troops in other countries' wars. The King of the German state Hesse-Cassel claimed that the hiring out of his army was his country's one resource. Throughout the first half of the eighteenth century there were 50,000 Swiss troops employed in other European armies. The trade in men at arms between European countries was a major element of European commerce and a significant influence in relations between states.

3 Discipline and Training

KEY ISSUE Why were discipline and training such important features of eighteenth-century armies?

The trend towards larger standing armies brought into the King's forces the reluctant, the kidnapped and the captured. Owing to the high rate of desertion men were placed under guard for their whole time in the army. For these men to be retained and to be made useful they had to be fiercely disciplined and trained. As Frederick the Great of Prussia said, 'They must be made to fear their officers more than danger... The slightest loosening of discipline would lead to barbarisation.'[2] The lash was a common form of punishment, even killing men in the process.

This level of enforcement was new, as earlier mercenary forces were notoriously ill-disciplined and independent. Typically they would refuse to do those jobs they considered beneath them, such as digging defences and trenches. The eighteenth-century commanders, however, required far greater control over their forces so that their men could be directed, without question, to perform all military duties. Unlike later generations, the fighting men of this period were not motivated by passionate causes such as nationalism, revolution or ideology. These unfortunates were largely unwilling participants who were only kept in place by the most ferocious discipline, brought about by drill, the continuous practice of marching, battle formations and weapon handling. In this way, the individual soldier became an unquestioning cog in the military machine, a 'walking musket'. These movements, practised on the parade ground and field, were to prepare men to hold positions in the face of deadly cavalry charge and close gunfire while still firing off the maximum force themselves. The most disciplined of armies, such as the Prussian, were likely to be the most successful. As the military commentator Turpin de Crissé observed in 1754, 'Battles are won not by numbers but by the manner of forming your troops together and their order and discipline.'[3]

The training of officers increased but it was patchy and half-hearted. With the growing awareness of the importance of artillery and its increasing sophistication there was an acceptance of the need for the effective training of artillery officers and engineers. Yet away from this specialist field, especially in the infantry and cavalry, officer training was sporadic and usually determined by the wealth and privilege of the officer's family.

4 The Weapons of War

> **KEY ISSUE** What were the most important weapons on the battlefield?

The weapons available to military forces are the chief determinant of tactics used. By today's standards, the pace of weapons development in this period appears virtually static, but warfare was transformed by significant improvements to the existing weapons of muskets and artillery at the end of the seventeenth century.

a) The Bayonet

The greatest change in the weaponry of land warfare in Europe at this time was the disappearance of the pike, the long, thrusting spear used by the foot soldier to repel attack by cavalry and opposing infantry. This cumbersome defensive instrument was now replaced by arming all infantrymen with a musket with a fitted bayonet. This apparently simple device represented a significant military breakthrough by expanding both the attacking and defensive capabilities of the infantry. Every infantryman was now both a pikeman and a musketeer. In defence there was no need for a separate pikeman to defend the musketeer against cavalry attack as each musket, now fitted with its own bayonet, enabled the infantryman to defend himself. The offensive capability of the infantry was also enhanced as pikemen were now transformed into musketeers, which increased firepower; and with bayonets fixed they could take part in deadly bayonet charges. Within two decades from 1690 all the major European armies had equipped their infantryman with this weapon. The early plug bayonets were fitted inside the barrel and obstructed firing, but the ring bayonet, which allowed free firing, soon replaced these.

b) Muskets

At the same time as the introduction of the bayonet the matchlock musket, ignited manually from a slow burning fuse, was replaced by the more reliable, and faster, flintlock musket, which produced its own spark. The flintlock muskets were lighter and therefore needed no prop or rest for the barrel. They could fire three rounds a minute, which represented a doubling of the previous rate of fire. The effect of both of these developments – the removal of a separate pikeman and the equipping of all infantrymen with the faster flintlock – was to dramatically increase firepower. Commanders could now make use of this greater firepower with longer lines of infantry on the battlefield to deliver it. As a result there was a corresponding increase in casualty rates with the majority of injuries now caused by gunfire rather than hand-to-hand combat. Yet despite these improvements muskets were still seriously limited in their effectiveness and reliability. The flintlock musket, like the preceding matchlock musket, was laboriously loaded down the barrel in a vulnerable standing position, and it was only accurate up to 100 yards. They had poor sights, inconsistent bullets and were prone to misfiring, overheating and breakdown. The newer rifled muskets had spiral grooves in the bore (the inside of the barrel), thus spinning the ball, which produced greater range and accuracy of up to 200 yards. However, these early rifles took twice as long to load, as the ball had to be forced down the muzzle against the rifled grooves, and they were twice as expensive to produce. As a result of these drawbacks rifles were only provided to a few sharpshooters/snipers amongst the light infantry until improvements in the nineteenth century increased their rate of fire and reduced production costs.

c) Artillery

The potential of artillery, when intelligently placed on the battlefield, had been demonstrated during the seventeenth century. The larger cannons had a range of 500 yards. They used heavy cannonballs against the reinforced walls of fortresses, and on the battlefield they could be even more devastating against the tightly packed infantry formations. Using grape shot (a bag of small shot) and canister (a tin or wooden cylinder of shot) to spread their fire, the cannons were effectively turned into a giant shotgun and sprayed the battlefield with a shower of deadly bullets or small shot. Canister proved to be the most effective anti-personnel weapon in use before the invention of shrapnel in the nineteenth century. It could sweep whole ranks of infantry off their feet, as the British discovered to their cost at Malplaquet (1709) and Dettingen (1743). Canister was the eighteenth-century equivalent of modern machine gun fire and by the middle of the century it was inflicting more casualties on the battlefield than any other weapon. However, the siting of the cannons was all-important, as they were too heavy to be moved during the course of a battle.

Slowly improvements were made to artillery, especially in regard to their mobility and flexibility. By the 1750s the resurgent Austrian army was using lighter cannon which were more manoeuvrable and could fire as rapidly as a musket. The French artillery made further refinements after 1765, making use of more advanced ironworking technology and standardised production. They were able to shorten the barrel without loss of range, and therefore cut the weight of the guns so that they could be moved more speedily by teams of horses, rather than oxen, to keep up with the infantry. Also, once on the battlefield, professional, highly trained gun crews could manoeuvre them more easily. Yet despite these improvements artillery units were still subject to many of the limitations that afflicted the musketeers. They too suffered from poor accuracy, backfiring and explosions in the muzzle, and they were usually firing blind, obscured by their own gun smoke and the thick 'fog of war' that hung over the battlefield.

5 The Tactics of War

KEY ISSUES Why did commanders try to avoid battles? When battles did occur, why was the infantry the most important force in the conflict?

By the beginning of the eighteenth century armies had grown in size, their capabilities were extended by training and they had increased their firepower and destructiveness by advances in artillery, muskets and the introduction of bayonets. Battlefield tactics now evolved to take account of the new possibilities of warfare. Battles could be hugely destructive of manpower and placed a massive financial burden on the king to fund replacements. Commanders therefore sought to avoid risking their forces in such ruinous encounters. As a result there emerged a 'twin-track' approach to tactics. Firstly the armies had to be prepared for full pitched battles but, in addition to this, there was a set of tactics to gain victories without battle. The idea was to keep the enemy on the move, not necessarily to annihilate but to exhaust him and his supplies, or to drive him into a hopeless position. Either of these tactics could result in retreat or surrender without a shot being fired. It was warfare of manoeuvre and counter-manoeuvre, of frontier fortresses and long sieges upon them. The 'War' of the Bavarian Succession (1778–9) between Austria and Prussia, for example, was contested between two armies of up to 200,000 men who managed never to meet in battle but manoeuvred each other into exhaustion, lack of supplies and deadlock.

Warfare was the most expensive activity a king could undertake and carried the risk of undermining his rule and destroying him. A long and costly war often defeated an opponent who had not been destroyed in battle. When an opponent ran out of money he had to surrender or negotiate. As J.F.C. Fuller puts it, 'Money, not blood, was the deciding factor.'[4] The American War of Independence cost the British government an unheard of £110 million and the same war bankrupted the French state and paved the way for revolution. Even Frederick the Great of Prussia, most remembered for his leadership in battles, wrote in his 'Instructions for his Generals' 1747: 'The greatest secret of war and the masterpiece of a skilful general is to starve his enemy. Hunger exhausts men more surely than courage, and you will succeed with less risk than by fighting.'[5]

a) Fortresses

The last quarter of the seventeenth century had seen the building of huge fortresses, especially on the French frontier. Fortresses had played a significant part in warfare as stores of food and supplies, and their establishment, was an indicator of control and domination; they fixed frontiers and were central to defence. This was particularly the case in Eastern Europe with its less permanent borders and its multinational empires. Fortresses, and fortified cities, could suck in the enemy attack, and their overthrow would require vast resources and time from their opponents. They played an important role in the wars of the early eighteenth century, but by the 1730s the fortress and siege warfare were losing their significance in European conflict.

Fortifications could not win a war; they were a drain on resources and were dependent on relieving forces if attacked. There continued to be examples of siege warfare throughout the century, but by the 1740s it was field armies and the battles between them that were dominant.

b) Infantry

The largest and most significant element of the dynastic armies was the highly trained infantry – the foot-soldiers or 'walking muskets.' More than three-quarters of the soldiers in royal armies were in the infantry. They were organised into manageable command sections with regiments of 1,600 men, divided into two battalions, each of which comprised eight companies. The battlefield experience for the infantry was truly horrifying: they had to stand their ground or advance slowly in close line formation across the battlefield to face the enemy. Owing to the inaccuracy of their muskets, they would have to close in on the enemy to less than 100 yards before firing. The close formation of infantry was designed to be a defence against cavalry attack and to maximise their firepower. Unfortunately, it also made them an alarmingly easy target for musket and cannon fire.

The muskets used were slow to load as the single shot had to be rammed down the length of the muzzle. This allowed only two or three shots per minute, which was significantly less than a skilled long-bow archer could fire centuries before, but commanders had developed linear tactics to overcome the slow rate of fire. The infantry units faced the enemy in long lines of men three rows deep. The men in the front line, on order, fired their round in unison, a volley of fire having, it was thought, greater psychological impact. The men in the row behind them would step forward and fire their volley, and a third row would then step through to fire theirs, to be replaced by the first line, who by now had reloaded. (Of course this complex operation was carried out while the enemy was blasting away at them from a distance of only a few dozen yards!) This rotating system of firing attempted to overcome the technical drawback of lengthy reloading. One man could only fire once every 20 to 30 seconds but a highly trained infantry company, synchronising their lines of fire, could deliver a devastating series of heavy volleys every few seconds. It was an operation which required great precision, timing and courage, for which the long hard years of training and discipline had prepared them. Yet only in a minority of cases could this parade ground order be maintained in the terror and confusion of battle for more than the first few volleys. The disciplined firing would usually collapse after the damage caused by the initial volleys to be followed by a desperate bayonet charge or an even speedier retreat.

The enormous firepower of muskets and artillery at close range on troops in tight formation meant that battles could sometimes be decided within half an hour, such as the British defeat of the French at Dettingen in 1743. With the possibility of battles being so quickly decided and so destructive of manpower, open conflict was avoided if at all possible, unless a commander believed his forces had a definite advantage in terms of numbers or superior position.

On either side of the main force were two smaller companies of light infantry and Grenadiers (the biggest men) to charge into the enemy with gun and bayonet: they were the shock troops of the eighteenth century. But generally, the infantry in combat were slow and immobile. The men took time to form into a line before battle and could advance only slowly to keep the line together: if it broke apart they would be in danger from charging cavalry. The uniforms of the infantry were bright and colourful so that commanders could keep them in view and, necessary in hand to hand fighting, identify the enemy amidst the thick acrid smoke from musket fire. Yet the vibrant uniforms also made the troops more of a target, and this, in addition to their slow manoeuvre and tight formation, meant that casualty rates from opposing musket and artillery-fire could be appalling.

After 1763 the European armies tried to incorporate some of the lessons provided by the Seven Years War. There was greater use of light infantry, especially by the French and British armies, and the beginnings of a move away from close formation tactics to the more flexible attacks of 'skirmishers' firing their more accurate rifles individually rather than in volleys.

c) Cavalry

The cavalry played a secondary role on the battlefield, although on occasions they could still have a significant impact on conflicts, especially on the more open plains of Eastern Europe. The organised firepower of artillery and infantry and the defensive power of the bayonet had robbed the cavalry of their pre-eminence in attack. The infantry battalion could defend itself against a cavalry charge by forming a hollow square/diamond formation with heavy guns at the corners. The combined firepower of these infantry units could bring down enough horses to stop the charge, and a tightly formed row of extended bayonets usually deterred any further advance. The most famous example of the resilience of these formations was the British squares which repelled Napoleon's cavalry at Waterloo in 1815. The cavalry's main responsibilities were reconnaissance and protecting the flanks of the infantry and artillery in battle if required. Cavalry was only sent into battle against other cavalry or if the enemy's infantry formations were in disarray.

d) Artillery

Tightly packed infantry formations may have been a defence against cavalry but they could be extremely vulnerable to artillery fire. The infantry units could not take cover on the battlefield as they had to load and fire their muskets in a standing position. When the infantry came within range of the artillery the effects were devastating, and could determine the outcome of an entire battle. The artillery was revealing its potential as the great destroyer on the battlefield. The greatest limitation on the effectiveness of the artillery in the early half of the century was their lack of mobility. The heavy guns were dragged into position by oxen and their civilian handlers before the battle and had to remain in that place. Despite this drawback the battlefield use of artillery grew substantially throughout the century, encouraged by technical modifications that increased its manoeuvrability and rate of fire.

6 Supplies

> **KEY ISSUE** How did the provision of supplies limit military activities?

A vital element of any campaign was the guaranteed provision of adequate supplies of food, fodder and ammunition for armies in excess of 50,000 men. Failure to meet this massive demand was one of the major constraints on military activity during this period. Without regular supplies an army's force was dissipated in the search for food, either to be seized or purchased. We can feel Frederick II's exasperation when he claimed 'It is not I who commands the army but flour and forage [who] are the masters.'[6] Supplies needed to be built up in the spring in fortresses or fortified cities on the frontier. The huge accumulation of fodder for horses ensured that operations could only begin in late spring and could not continue beyond the end of the growing season. Furthermore the debilitating effect of autumn floods and winter freezes on primitive communications meant that warfare was generally a seasonal activity, limited to late spring and summer. Commanders had to calculate very carefully the operations they could fit into the brief 'campaigning season': a long siege could take up all of that year's available activity and might still not produce a successful result. Success in war was usually made up of a series of incremental advances over a number of seasons rather than single decisive battles.

One of the most significant changes in the nature of warfare in the eighteenth century was the move towards the guaranteed provision of supplies. With assured supplies armies had less need to pillage, and the host population was less likely to be terrorised for their food stocks. Wars in previous centuries had often degenerated into vicious struggles over food supplies, and the greatest victim of these wars was the civilian population. Now, for the more prosperous and organised states such as France, campaigns were mounted from their supply bases at fortresses. Beyond this, storage depots or magazines were established at regular points to act as staging posts for supplies to armies in the field. Despite this improvement, however, the daunting logistical problem of organising supplies, and their cost, placed an upper limit of 50,000 to 70,000 on the size of armies in the field and acted as a severe restraint on the range and impact of military operations.

7 Leadership

> **KEY ISSUES** What impact did military commanders have on battles in this century? What were the strengths and weaknesses of Frederick the Great as a military leader?

a) The Nature of Military Leadership in the Eighteenth Century

In the age of absolute monarchs the command of armies, like foreign policy, was the prerogative of the king. The monarch would normally devolve the power of command down to one of his (younger) relatives or to an aristocratic general, but it was still not unusual for a king to take personal command of his country's military operations. Despite a reputation for cautious and limited military commanders, the eighteenth century produced a number of outstanding leaders, such as the Duke of Marlborough during the War of the Spanish Succession (1701–1714) and from the middle of the century Marshal Saxe, the French commander, and Frederick the Great of Prussia.

Despite these examples the impact of leadership during the course of a battle must be treated with some caution. Once a battle was under way there was remarkably little a commander could do. In the thick of battle, in so far as the conflict could be managed at all, it was the responsibility of the subordinate officers. Even then the infantry officers were simply following the dictates of a rigid, prearranged plan. During the battle the most that the general could do was to decide when to order his reserve troops into the conflict. If the commander had a limited impact on the course of the battle he had a greater responsibility in the preparation for combat. Frederick the Great devised new tactics and personally supervised and inspected training grounds. Marlborough's victory at Blenheim in 1704 was secured as much by ensuring supplies for his army's 250 mile march to the battlefield as events on it. But the greatest responsibility of the commander was to decide how, when, where and if, the battle would be fought. At this stage he had to take into account factors that would be recognisable to generals throughout the ages. These were the vital calculations about an enemy's strength, the freshness and morale of one's own forces, and the advantages of terrain.

b) An Example of Leadership: Frederick the Great

Frederick the Great, as he became known, was the purest example of
the soldier-king, and the most successful. Frederick became King of
Prussia in October 1740, aged 28, and transformed the small, frag-
mented Prussian state of 2.5 million people into a great power via the
army. To strengthen Prussia's position Frederick immediately
expanded the army and seized the adjoining wealthy Austrian
province of Silesia. After the ensuing Silesian Wars Prussia retained
the conquest until 1756, when a seemingly overwhelming coalition of
Russia, Austria, France, Saxony, Poland and Sweden was formed to
reclaim Silesia and break up Prussia itself. This was the ultimate test
for Frederick: the very survival of Prussia was at stake. In the following
Seven Years War he confirmed his status as one of the great commanders. To defend Prussia, and its Silesian conquest, he split his
armies to strike against his foes individually, to prevent united action.
By military or diplomatic means Frederick picked off his enemies one
by one.

The dominant feature of Frederick's style of war, which set him
apart from the defensive, limited tactics of his contemporaries, was his
determination to attack, even against superior numbers. He was also
prepared to risk a far higher casualty rate for his own forces than was
considered acceptable for the time. Apart from the exceptions of
Rossbach and Leuthen,-in every battle fought by Frederick II, what-
ever the outcome, the Prussians sustained greater casualties than
their opponents. Frederick's tactical innovation was designed to harness this aggression and bring mobility and decisiveness back to the
battlefield. He had the advantage of the most highly trained of
Europe's armies in terms of their faster marching and firing speeds,
and his tactics sought to make full use of these assets. His solution, the
'oblique tactic', was to strengthen one wing of his infantry so that, in
perfect marching order, it could out-flank and surround the enemy's
wing. To succeed the attack on the wing had to be disguised, and then
executed with speed and discipline, to prevent any defensive
measures to counter it.

During the Seven Years War Frederick perfected the oblique order
of battle, its most spectacular success being the battle of Rossbach,
November 1757. Here in less than three hours the Prussians killed or
captured 16,000 French troops for the loss of just 500 of their own
men and effectively expelled France from the war. Napoleon later
commented, 'That battle was a masterpiece. Of itself it is sufficient to
entitle Frederick to a place in the first rank among generals.'

Against these achievements must be weighed the limitations of
Frederick's leadership. He suffered a number of costly defeats and
the death rate among his troops was staggering. The Prussian soldiers
fighting in the Seven Years War had only a one in 15 chance of survival. His tactical innovations were short-lived, as opponents could

counter them once they had witnessed them. Also Frederick made no effort to prepare his successor and he refused to modernise his forces and tactics after 1763. On his insistence the organisation of the army remained tied to its structure of the 1730s and its tactics therefore became increasingly predictable and outdated. Rival kingdoms that had struggled to match Prussian efficiency now surpassed it and showed far greater flexibility on the battlefield.

8 Conclusion: Limited Warfare?

> **KEY ISSUE** Why has the eighteenth century been described as the age of 'limited warfare'?

The term most commonly applied to warfare in the eighteenth century is 'limited'. The period is usually portrayed as an age of restrained warfare between rival kings, fought for limited objectives rather than the complete destruction of their opponents. Warfare was also limited in its impact on the civilian population, with soldiers deliberately distanced from civilians during both war and peace. During peacetime the men at arms were quartered separately in barracks and were paid, supplied and fed by the king to prevent the violent exploitation of the host population, and to minimise the risk of desertion. In wartime, despite the fact that the armies were bigger than before, they were correspondingly more controlled and disciplined so that casualties were confined mostly to the fighting forces. Organised supplies removed the need for pillage from the civilian population. The marked reduction in civilian casualties represents a central feature of limited warfare.

The reason for this restraint was both moral and economic. In moral terms there was a general acceptance of the need for a civilised code of behaviour for the conduct of war. This arose from two sources: firstly, a revulsion against the horrors of unlimited warfare as demonstrated by the religious struggles of the Thirty Years War (1618–48), and secondly, the humanising influence of the ideas of the Enlightenment. Kings, such as Frederick II, now fought for limited, material goals such as a fortress, a slice of territory or a colony, not for ideological causes and the complete annihilation of their enemy. Europe had learnt the hard way that questions of religion would not be settled on the battlefield. Adding material weight to the new morality was the cost factor. The economic motivation for restraint in war was obvious: the funding of the king's army was hugely expensive and consumed the majority of the state's finances. Battlefield casualty rates of up to 30 per cent in a single day, and the subsequent cost of replacements, could be ruinous. Commanders were made aware of the need to prevent such expensive losses by avoiding battle for as long as possible.

Apart from the conscious restraint of the kings there were also practical constraints over which the monarchs had no control. Improved weaponry had the potential to be more effective and destructive, but at this early stage of industrial development it was severely inhibited by its technical deficiencies and unreliability. Armies increased in size but were continually degraded by the high level of losses due to disease, desertion and death in battle, and were dependent on inexperienced and unreliable replacements. Military operations were confined in their range by the speed and distance that a fully laden soldier could march over open ground and the even slower pace of supply wagons to reach him. Even this restricted mobility was only possible in late spring and summer. The lack of an effective communication system to overcome the obstacles of distance and climate was probably the greatest restraint on the impact of armies in the eighteenth century.

These limitations, and the slow rate of technological development, have led many writers to regard warfare in the century as limited in its aims and methods, and inconsequential in its results. They point to the fact that even when battles did occur, and a clear victory was achieved, it rarely decided the outcome of wars. Russell Weigley describes the period of prolonged, indecisive wars as 'a history of almost unbroken futility.'[7]

Yet this view does not sufficiently take into account the far-reaching consequences for the European balance of power brought about by warfare. During this period French dominance was thwarted, Prussia established itself as a great power, the Turks were largely repelled from Central and Eastern Europe, and Russian power grew significantly. Also, we must keep in mind the impact of war, and the preparation for war, on the European states and their people. Many states were transformed and modernised by the establishment of large standing armies. The first modern bureaucracies had been called into being to finance and run the armies, whole societies had been remodelled for war and new militaristic values had been spread through all levels of society. The practice of warfare may have been limited, but its impact and consequences undoubtedly were not.

References

1   Michael Howard, *War in European History* (Oxford, 1976), p. 66.
2   J.F.C. Fuller, *The Conduct of War 1789–1961* (Da Capo, 1992), p. 21.
3   Geoffrey Treasure, *The Making of Modern Europe* (Methuen, 1985), p. 209.
4   Fuller, *Conduct of War*, p. 24.
5   T.R. Phillips, *The Roots of Strategy* (Greenwood, 1940), p. 213.
6   J. Luvaas, *Frederick the Great on the Art of War* (De Capo, 1999), p. 16.
7   R. Weigley, *The Age of Battles* (Pimlico, 1991), p. xiii.

Summary Diagram
Warfare in the Eighteenth Century

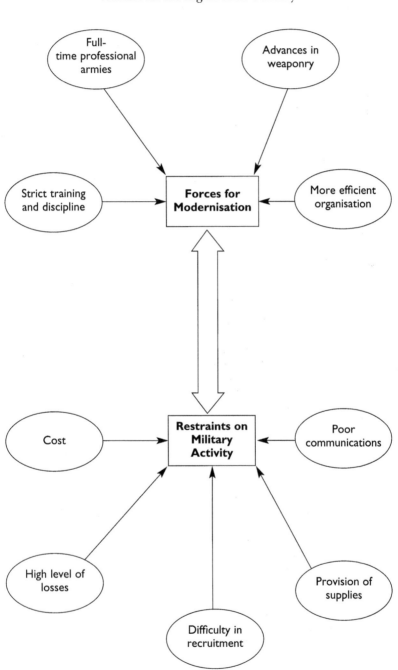

Answering structured and essay questions on Chapter 2

Structured questions present you with two or three part questions. The early question(s) appear to be easier as they ask for a factual account; the last question often builds upon the information you provided in your first answer and demands a more analytical explanation. The final question will also earn the majority of marks and you must devote the majority of your time to it. Try the following example:

a) Explain how the cost of war and the under-developed nature of weapons technology restricted the impact of warfare in the eighteenth century. *(20 marks)*

b) To what extent is it true to say that the eighteenth century up to 1792 was the age of limited warfare? *(40 marks)*

Question (a) is asking you to focus on two of the reasons for constraints on warfare in this period. Question (b) follows the same issue but asks you to expand it into a wider debate on the validity of the term 'limited warfare'.

One tip to remember here is that any question that opens with the words 'To what extent ...' or 'How far ...' is often known as a 'yes ... but' question. This is because it will nearly always be the case that there is a lot of truth in the statement but there will also be reservations or objections against it. Your answer must reflect both sides of this issue. Always give thought to the structure of your answer and sketch this out in rough before you start.

Obviously the key term in this question is 'limited warfare': therefore start off with a definition of what this is so that you can give an informed judgement on how far it existed. Then provide an explanation of all of the factors which limited war. For example: primitive transport and communications, winter weather, the cost of training and replacing armies, the state of weapons technology, the high level of losses to armies, and the moral restraint of the kings to avoid unnecessary deaths especially among civilians. Follow this up with objections to the validity of the term 'limited warfare'. You could include such factors as: increased death rates in battle (e.g. the Seven Years War), and the continuation of barbaric action in war, and towards civilians (especially in Eastern Europe). You could also mention the far-reaching consequences of war, which again challenge the notion of limited warfare. For example: the decisive shifts in the European balance of power and the transforming effect of warfare on states and society.

Examples of essay questions include the following:

1. 'A history of almost unbroken futility.' How accurately does this comment reflect the nature and impact of war in the period 1700–1792?

2. 'Frederick II proves that leadership is the most decisive element in the conduct of war.' How far do you agree with this comment in the context of the period 1700–1792?

3. To what extent does Frederick II deserve the title 'Frederick the Great' in regard to his military leadership?

Questions 1 and 2 present you with a challenging statement which you must respond to directly. This is a common form of question, which does not necessarily expect you to agree with the statement; but you must provide a balanced account of the various interpretations of the debate. For question 1 you can use the same information as you used for b) in the structured questions. The opening statement is referring to the limitations on warfare and the lack of decisive victories on the battlefield. Outline this argument before providing the other side of the debate. The statement in question 2 stresses the importance of one of the characteristics of warfare, i.e. leadership, over all the others. Respond to the statement by outlining the achievements of Frederick II but then you can balance this by pointing out his deficiencies as a leader and the limited impact that all leaders had on the conduct of war in this period. Also emphasise the importance of the other elements of warfare: organisation, supplies, a trained professional army, weaponry, as well as finance and resources. Question 3 requires a balanced evaluation of Frederick's military leadership before you provide your judgement in the conclusion.

The Wars of Revolution: The Challenge to the Kings

3

POINTS TO CONSIDER

Chapter two presented the basic characteristics of eighteenth-century warfare and provided us with a framework against which we can assess the degree of change and continuity in later periods of warfare. Developments in the French Wars represent significant progress towards modern warfare. You need to be clear about those areas of change and what factors brought them about at this particular time. Also you must keep in mind those continuing limitations on the exercise of war.

KEY DATES

1775–1783		The American War of Independence.
1789		The beginning of the French Revolution.
1792	**April**	France declares war on Austria.
1793	**January**	Execution of the French king.
1793		First coalition formed against France.
1793	**August 23**	Decree of *levée en masse* raises one million men.
1795		The revolutionary armies are directed outwards for foreign conquest.
1796		Napoleon appointed commander of Army of Italy.
1798–1802		Second coalition against France.
1799		Napoleon becomes First Consul.
1804		Napoleon proclaimed Emperor of the French.
1805		Third coalition.
1805		Napoleonic victories at Ulm and Austerlitz but defeat at Trafalgar.
1806		Continental blockade against British goods introduced.
1807–13		The Spanish ulcer, Napoleon's unsuccessful attempt to subdue Spain.
1812		Napoleon's invasion of Russia.
1813		Fourth coalition; the Battle of Nations (Leipzig); invasion of France.
1814		Paris falls; Napoleon abdicates, exiled to Elba.
1815		Napoleon escapes from Elba, defeated at Waterloo.

1 Introduction

KEY ISSUE Why were the wars of the American and French Revolutions such a departure from the wars of the kings?

The first break from the wars of the kings were the wars of revolution, the American and French revolutions. They were waged against the armies of the kings and they were fought for ideas, like independence, liberty or the export of revolution to other countries. America's War of Independence, successfully concluded by January 1783, was the first national war of modern times. Her armed forces had largely been drawn from volunteers and local militia, and had often used tactics that departed from the eighteenth-century European model. Yet despite these indicators of modern warfare the American War of Independence made little impact on the European conduct of war. It was largely seen as a small-scale, remote, colonial insurgency with little relevance to the European theatre of war. The wars of the French Revolution, however, signified national war on a massive scale and changed the nature of warfare fundamentally. Many of the features we now recognise as modern warfare – mass armies and mass casualties, the vast scale of war, the mobilisation of whole populations – arose during the French wars. Revolutionary and Napoleonic France led the way, sweeping aside the old order of kings and their armies. To meet the challenge, the kings and emperors of Europe had to copy the French in terms of the size and tactics of their armies and the militarisation of their societies.

2 The Defence of the Revolution: The Nation in Arms

> **KEY ISSUE** How did the revolution lead to a Nation in Arms?

The French Revolution represented a radical transformation of the social and political foundations of the French kingdom; the French army, as a reflection of that society, was equally transformed. The primary aim of eighteenth-century armies was to preserve the monarch in absolute authority. Clearly the French military, driven by the same passions and divisions as other sections of society, had been unable to perform this basic duty. The regular army, with its politically suspect aristocratic officer class, was downgraded and swamped by a huge volunteer National Guard formed to protect the revolution. As aristocratic officers fled, or were dismissed, so younger, politically motivated officers drawn from the middle class replaced them. In September 1791 the army was stripped of its title of 'Royal' and the new military oath made no reference to the king. The message was clear: the army was no longer the personal possession of the king to fight his personal disputes. A call for volunteers in 1791 and 1792, and limited conscription in the same year, temporarily shored up a disintegrating army. But by the summer of 1792 France faced widespread uprisings at home and war with Austria and Prussia, who felt the need to champion the anti-revolutionary cause. Revolutionary France, from a position of extreme weakness, grandly proclaimed its willingness to 'assist all peoples who seek to recover their liberty'. For conservative, royalist Europe this was final proof that revolutionary and, by now, republican France was throwing out a challenge to the existing order with its intention to export the revolution. Europe responded by forming the 'first coalition' against the renegade state.

Civil war, foreign invasion and widespread desertion from the revolutionary armies forced the ruling Convention into a last desperate act, the militarisation of the entire nation. On 23 August 1793 this was put into practice by the historic decree of the *levée en masse*:

1   From this time, until the enemies of France have been expelled from the territory of the Republic, all Frenchmen are in a state of permanent requisition for the army. The young men will go to fight; married men will forge arms and transport food and supplies; women will make tents and 5   uniforms and work in hospitals; children will find old rags for bandages; old men will appear in public places to excite the courage of warriors, the hatred of kings, and the unity of the Republic.

Public buildings will be converted into barracks, public squares into armament workshops, the soil of cellars will be washed to extract salt-10 petre.

Riding horses will be requisitioned for the cavalry corps; draught horses, other than those used in agriculture, will pull artillery and stores.

The Committee of Public Safety is charged with the taking of all 15 measures to establish, without delay, an extraordinary factory for arms of all kinds ... as well as requiring, for this purpose, throughout the Republic, craftsmen and workers who can contribute to its success ...

This was not just a call to arms; it was the calling up of the entire nation. The *levée* raised an army of over a million men and, as a result, radically altered the nature of warfare. The degree of ideological and military mobilisation was unprecedented, laying the foundations for a total war effort not to be seen in Europe again for another 100 years. Under the pressure of inflamed public opinion on one side and the threat of the guillotine on the other, revolutionary France transformed itself into the 'Nation-in-Arms' that was to sweep all before it for 20 years.

3 Total War

> **KEY ISSUE** How was French society organised for a total war
> effort?

At the end of 1792 France had thrown down a challenge to all of royalist Europe but without the military means to do anything about it. With the *levée en masse* it had raised an army that might fulfil that challenge, but French society had to transform itself to arm, clothe and supply this astonishing force. The effort could only be achieved through ruthless discipline and totalitarian control. This was notoriously provided by the Committee of Public Safety (CPS), and its military section, which was headed by the highly effective Lazare Carnot. In 1793–4 Carnot restored some military order by amalgamating the volunteer forces with the regular army. To oversee every action of the generals, and to supervise the political indoctrination of the troops, the CPS appointed 'deputies on mission'. As their directive of 14 December chillingly put it, 'We have noted that success has always followed obedience of the committee's orders and that defeats have stemmed from their neglect. Generals! the time of disobedience is over'. Defeat, hesitation, or perceived political unreliability now meant death. In 1793 17 generals were publicly executed, and in 1794 a further 67 met the same fate.

The same degree of discipline was imposed on the civilian population in the period that became known as 'The Terror'. The economic resources of France were fully mobilised to supply their mass army – a logistical nightmare considering the fact that the republican army was more than ten times the size of the average eighteenth-century army. The priority of course was weapons. The CPS quickly established 20 new sword and bayonet factories and 12 new gun factories, the biggest of which, in Paris, produced as many muskets as the rest of Europe put together. Transport and industry were nationalised and made to serve the war effort. Rigid price controls were imposed as well as the wholesale requisitioning of labour, property and produce. Non-compliance with government regulations led to the guillotine. Never before had a government commanded so much power.

Clausewitz, the military theorist, observed at the time that

1   a force appeared that beggared all imagination. Suddenly war again
     became the business of the people – a people of thirty millions, all of
     whom considered themselves to be citizens ... The people became a
     participant in war; instead of governments and armies as heretofore,
5   the full weight of the nation was thrown into the balance. The
     resources and efforts now available for use surpassed all conventional
     limits: nothing now impeded the vigour with which war could be
     waged.[1]

4 The Art of Revolutionary Warfare: Tactics and Effectiveness

KEY ISSUE How did the revolutionary commanders adapt their tactics and organisation to make best use of their large, untrained armies?

In early 1792 the revolutionary army was considered a shambles both at home and abroad. In its first battle in April near Valenciennes it surprised nobody when it ran away, lynching its commander on the way. Yet by 1794 it had driven all of its enemies from French soil, at the same time as fighting a bitter civil war. By 1796, before Napoleon had made an impact, the French revolutionaries had raised, and armed, the largest army Europe had ever seen, and used it to extend French territory to an extent not witnessed for many decades. The revolutionary armies brought about a revolution in warfare every bit as significant as that ushered in by Napoleon. How had this remarkable transformation come about?

The radical changes in the art of war introduced by the revolutionaries were not totally novel. The revolution inherited reforms and new ideas proposed in the last years of the monarchy. With a newer, more experimental leadership, France was prepared to act on these ideas. Perhaps the most useful inheritance for the revolution was the reform of French artillery under the direction of Jean de Gribeauval from the 1760s onwards. Gribeauval standardised the calibre and ammunition of the French cannon, making them more mobile and more accurate. The rate of fire was also improved and it was proposed that the cannons should be grouped together in highly effective batteries to concentrate their fire. The artillery passed down to the French revolution was the most advanced in the world.

a) Divisions

Another reform that had begun in the last years of the monarchy was the reorganisation of the cumbersome old regimental army into manoeuvrable 'divisions' of 12,000 men that combined infantry, cavalry and artillery in single fighting units. The divisional system produced greater speed and flexibility of movement, and allowed armies to expand as they could draw their supplies from different areas of the country. The divisions could make their own way to the battlefield to fall upon the enemy from different, and unexpected, directions. Carnot speeded up the institution of divisions and their convergence on the battlefield, but this remained a hit-and-miss affair for the revolutionary armies. It was not until Napoleon's greater military and political control over resources that we see the stunning battlefield successes of the co-ordinated divisional system.

b) Shock Tactics

The greatest motivation for tactical change was simple necessity. The new mass armies raised by the revolutionaries were quickly thrown into the conflict with barely any training. As a consequence the drilled, disciplined infantry, the mainstay of the eighteenth-century army, was no longer available to the revolutionary armies. Carnot and the army commanders therefore made a virtue out of necessity by adopting 'shock tactics'. Since their largely untrained troops had no hope of outfiring the professional infantry lines of their opponents, their only alternative was to storm the enemy troops in a blood-curdling bayonet charge before too many of them were cut down by enemy fire. As Carnot urged, 'No more manoeuvres, no more military art but fire, steel and patriotism … We must exterminate, exterminate to the bitter end'. This was the death knell for the ideals and restraints of the limited warfare of the eighteenth century.

c) Reorganisation

Carnot and the French commanders reorganised their forces to support shock tactics. To present less of a target to the opposing infantry and artillery the French troops were compressed into attack columns of around 50 to 80 men across the front, and nine to 12 men deep. The columns were not arranged for firepower, they represented a crude, powerful human battering ram to charge at the enemy and break their thin line formation. The men in the columns would sprint as fast as they could across the battlefield but the well drilled, professional soldiers of the coalition were able to inflict enormous casualties on them. The revolutionary armies would routinely suffer 20 per cent casualties in their repeat attacks. The smaller, old style allied armies could not sustain such losses and would often give way even though they had inflicted more casualties on their opponent. The French armies tried to provide what cover they could for their vulnerable columns by softening up the enemy beforehand with an artillery barrage and the sniping of skirmishers. By costly trial and error, losing as many battles as they won, the French armies in 1795 had evolved a flexible 'mixed order' of linear formations, attack columns, skirmishing and sniping. By 1795, given their numbers, their enthusiasm and their battle-hardened experience, they had grown into the most powerful, menacing army in the world.

d) Numbers

The key to the new French way of war, the engine which drove the French war machine, was not tactics, nor leadership, it was the unprecedented number of men they were able to mobilise. Their bloodthirsty tactics (which nearly always produced far more French casualties than allied ones) were only feasible because the levies of 1793, and continued conscription thereafter, provided commanders with a seemingly inexhaustible supply of replacements. With 30 million citizens to draw upon, France was the second most populous country in Europe, only narrowly behind Russia. The French revolutionary armies were many times larger than their opponents' forces; they could simply afford more losses than the allies. The huge losses in the revolutionary wars were not caused by individual battles but by the incredible number of them. In 1793, at the height of the conflict, French forces were engaged in ten separate campaigns simultaneously. Worldwide, this represented two to three battles per week! Under pressure of almost continuous combat the under-strength coalition forces were driven out of France, the Austrian Netherlands and the Rhineland.

5 The Wars of Conquest and the Revolution in Supplies

> **KEY ISSUES** What were the improvements in agriculture and transport which supported mass armies on the move? How was the civilian brought back into warfare?

The revolution had been defended by its huge patriotic army and a total war effort, but it could not end there: the revolution was driven on by its own military force. By 1795 the French army had expelled the last of the foreign invaders. This massive army could not be returned to civilian life without producing chaos in France; the country could not support the army, and therefore it was set loose on foreign powers. The war, which had begun as the defence of France and the revolution, was now turned into one of foreign conquest and plunder.

a) The Revolution in Supplies: Removing the 'Leg Irons'

The logistical problem of supplying armies in the field was one of the greatest restraints on the scope and size of armies in the eighteenth century. The cost and the difficulties in the physical supply of armies had constrained their movement and generally limited their size to an upper limit of 50,000 to 70,000. No wonder the French reformer Guibert referred to supply lines as 'leg irons'. The French had exploded that upper limit with their revolutionary mass army, but it required a corresponding revolution in the provision of supplies to sustain these forces. The only solution was a complete break with the eighteenth-century practice of guaranteed supply convoys and depots, and a return to the earlier practice of living off the land. The troops were left to their own devices with the instruction to 'nourish war with war'. The change in the system of supplies represents a paradox in the development of warfare. To release the potential of their more modern mass army the revolutionaries and Napoleon had to revert to a more primitive system of foraging. Up until 1795 the burden of requisition, enforced by revolutionary discipline, fell upon the French civilian and helped to play its part in the rural uprisings. After this date foreigners, both rich and poor, were made to pay the costs of the French army and to feed them. One French officer wrote: 'Our expedition [across] the Rhine was due entirely to pecuniary considerations ... Our incursion into a rich and defenceless country was to procure us the money of which we were in such dire need.'[2]

b) The Involvement of the Civilian

The consequences of this development were profound. The limited wars of the eighteenth century had tried to protect the civilian population from the worst effects of war. The wars of the French Revolution and Napoleon now drew the civilian, his home and possessions, into the very centre of the conflict. The results for the civilians could be devastating. In 1793 a French officer in Germany admitted, 'From time to time we would make expeditions into enemy territory ... we would fall suddenly on a village which we would devastate. We loaded the wagons with all we could find ... the peasants were abused, sometimes killed; the women raped; everything was permitted.'[3] This practice did not noticeably change under Napoleon's leadership. The brutal exploitation of the civilian population had an important military consequence as it led to determined resistance movements and guerrilla war in occupied territories, most damagingly in Spain. The Duke of Wellington, by contrast, ensured that supplies drawn from the locality were paid for and the conduct of the British troops was carefully supervised. As a result Wellington's forces could usually count on more civilian co-operation than those of Napoleon.

c) The Impact of the Agricultural Revolution

The mass revolutionary and Napoleonic armies could not have supported themselves in this exploitative fashion in any previous age, as the basic foodstuffs would not have been available. The French armies were sustained by the fruits of an agricultural revolution that had taken place in the latter decades of the eighteenth century, especially in the main campaigning areas of northern Europe and northern Italy. This revolution had, for the first time, led to sizeable agricultural surpluses and the greater cultivation of root vegetables, in particular the potato. It was these surpluses which fed the mass armies on the move. For Napoleon the return to the system of forage was essential. The speed with which he drove his armies, and the distances they covered, made it impossible for their supply convoy to reach them. The resort to forage and requisition made possible Napoleon's huge, rapid armies that transformed the military balance of power. The advantages conferred by this system of warfare were immense but it also contained inherent weaknesses and dangers. Napoleon's armies rapidly exhausted the land they occupied; they could only replenish their supplies by moving on or capturing enemy supply depots. The developed lands of Western Europe could sustain his mass armies in this fashion, but once Napoleon entered the less fertile territories of Spain and Poland in 1807, he was presented with supply problems he could not resolve. The greatest catastrophe to be inflicted on Napoleon's forces due to lack of supplies was the ill-fated invasion of Russia in 1812. The Russians used their vast landmass to fall back, drawing Napoleon's forces in beyond the range of their supply convoys, and then denying him the possibility of forage by destroying all means of sustenance and shelter. Of the 500,000 men who invaded Russia only 30,000 returned.

The agricultural revolution of the late eighteenth century bequeathed another asset to the expansionist French armies. The transport of surplus foodstuffs to markets and towns had created many more reliable, all-weather roads, at least in the wealthier areas of the continent. The dream of a widely dispersed, self-sustaining divisional system rapidly converging on the battlefield now became a reality. To fully exploit the potential for greater speed of movement, and a reflection of the shortage of supplies, the French armies reduced the vast amount of baggage that was usually carried by a campaigning army. Thus the French armies abandoned the use of tents, with both officers and men sleeping in the open at night (with a correspondingly sharp rise in the sickness rate). The advantage to the French in greater mobility and speed was dramatic, so much so that one by one the allies were forced to adopt the French system of reduced baggage trains and the discomfort of sleeping in the open.

6 Napoleon's Art of War

KEY ISSUES What was the significance of the 'decisive battle' and the corps system in Napoleon's style of war? Why did Napoleon's tactics become less sophisticated and less effective as the wars progressed?

As we have seen, the main elements and techniques of 'Napoleonic warfare' were already in place before Bonaparte made his successful entry on the scene with his dramatic Italian campaign. Napoleon does not represent a break with the revolutionaries' style of war, nor even that of the more progressive thinkers and reformers of the *ancien régime* (the old regime). Napoleon's genius was in combining the most inspired theories of the earlier reformers with the hard-won practical experience of the revolutionary armies.

a) Napoleon's Strategy

Napoleon's primary strategic aim was the quickest possible destruction of the enemy forces. The means to achieve this was to bring about the decisive battle to break the enemy army and remove further resistance. As Napoleon said, 'There are in Europe many good generals, but they see too many things at once. I see only one thing, namely the enemy's main body. I try to crush it.' This strategy, however, was forced upon Napoleon by the nature of his military forces. His large armies were a considerable advantage but they could only be fed by requisition and forage and they rapidly exhausted the territory they occupied. His forces had to move fast and bring their campaigns to a speedy conclusion. Hence the need to provoke the decisive encounter. This, of course, was a reversal of the eighteenth-century style of warfare with its strategy of manoeuvre to avoid battle. Napoleon sought to achieve the decisive battle by sending his strongest possible force so deep into enemy territory that it could not be ignored but had to be confronted. Napoleon then threatened the enemy force at its most vulnerable point: their lines of supply. One of the most successful examples of this strategy was the crushing defeat of Prussia at the twin battles of Jena-Auerstadt in October 1806. Napoleon drew the Prussians into battle by sending a huge force of 180,000 men towards Berlin, a challenge and threat to which the Prussians had to respond. The same principle lay behind his mass invasion of Russia in 1812. But the Russians were able to deny Napoleon his decisive battle, even allowing him to occupy a burnt-out Moscow. The Russians were able to trade space for time; the Russians had the space but Napoleon, without assured supplies in a hostile environment, did not have time.

b) Innovation: The Corps

One of Napoleon's first, and most successful, innovations was the introduction of the army corps made up of, on average, three infantry divisions, a cavalry brigade and 46 guns. The corps built on the success of the divisional system, but at 30,000 troops it was three times the strength. The corps was a big enough tactical unit to fight on its own but it was primarily designed for combined action with other corps, to strike at the enemy with great force from different directions. The army's effective range was massively expanded as a series of interrelated corps could be dispersed across hundreds of miles for forage yet could quickly converge for united action. The corps system built on one of the greatest strengths of the French armies compared to the allies, that of speed and mobility. The most outstanding demonstration of the corps system in action was in 1805 when the army was dispersed over a 200-mile front and with perfect timing encircled the bewildered Austrian army at Ulm. The corps then again separated, to bear down on the combined Austrian and Russian army at Austerlitz, who were routed with the loss of 30,000 men. The co-ordination and timing required to achieve such results, especially in an age of primitive communications, were phenomenal and arguably the greatest of Napoleon's many abilities. His masterful use of army corps and divisions revolutionised the whole technique of strategic movement, and became the model adopted for all modern armies.

c) Tactics

Bonaparte's preferred tactic, made possible by the corps system, was for his leading corps to pin down the enemy from the front while other units would outflank the enemy and attack in the rear. The slower moving allied army was thus encircled, as if caught in a net, and forced to surrender, as at Ulm, or face destruction. If the enemy was a larger force Napoleon would strike at the point at which the allied armies joined to divide his opponents, finish off the weaker link, and then turn his full strength on the remaining unit. Once battle commenced Napoleon's tactics were refinements of revolutionary warfare. His preferred infantry formation was the mixed order of lines of fire, attack columns and skirmishers. Artillery and skirmishers would attempt to break up the enemy lines before heavy infantry columns of several thousand men would each be sent in to uncover the weakest point. Once this weakness was revealed the mobile artillery was drawn up to concentrate their bombardment on that point, then fresh reserves (the Imperial Guard) would be thrown in to achieve breakthrough. Once the enemy had been routed, for final victory, the cavalry would lead the pursuit of the enemy hacking at the defeated, fleeing army. This could be the decisive, finishing blow on the opponent. It was most famously illustrated by the bloody pursuit of the Prussian army following their defeat at Jena-Auerstadt. Here the Prussians lost at least three times as many men in the 200-mile, two-week pursuit of their bedraggled army as they lost in the battle itself.

As the wars wore on, the quality of the conscripts and their level of training deteriorated and began to limit Napoleon's tactical options. Many of his troops were unable to manoeuvre on the battlefield and barely able to handle a musket. After 1807 Napoleon, like his revolutionary predecessors, had to fall back on crude attack columns which were thrown at the enemy lines, leading to even higher casualty rates. Another response to the general decline of the French forces was to increase the number of guns in the artillery batteries, and to use them heavily to pave the way for an assault. Napoleon attempted to replace guns for men. The French armies, apart from the legendary Imperial Guard, were less of a force on the battlefield, their aura of invincibility and their self-confidence drained away. Their tactics and movement, once so dazzling, had now become predictable. As Wellington said of the French tactics at Waterloo, 'They came on in the same old way and we stopped them in the same old way'.

d) Napoleon's Armies

In 1799 Napoleon inherited from the revolution a huge, but dispirited and poorly supplied force of 230,000. From this point on he brilliantly imposed his own personality on the army, generating a fierce loyalty and sense of purpose. During the period 1800–1815 1.5 million men were enlisted from France with at least half that number becoming casualties. In addition to this were large numbers of foreigners who volunteered or more often were part of an 'agreed' contribution of men from conquered or allied countries, especially from the German states. When the Grand Army gathered for the invasion of Russia in 1812 fewer than half of the 612,000 troops were French. The inclusion of such large numbers of reluctant or half-hearted soldiers was a major factor in the decline of the army's effectiveness. It is estimated that 400,000 of these foreign troops, about half of those who fought, died in the service of Napoleon's ambition.

7 The Scale and Intensity of the Wars – the Birth of Modern Warfare?

> **KEY ISSUES** What features of modern warfare can be detected in the Napoleonic wars? What features were absent?

a) The Scale of War

Compared with the limited conflicts of the eighteenth century, the French Wars were conducted on quite a different level. Napoleon's campaigns swept across continents, from Egypt to Spain to Russia. Beyond their European struggle Britain and France fought each other for worldwide colonial dominance, drawing Britain into another war with the United States. Because of this P. Fregosi in *Dreams of Empire* makes a strong claim for the French Wars to be considered the first genuine world war. In a number of other respects the wars, especially in their later stages, demonstrate many of the features of modern warfare. Following the French resort to the nation-in-arms, the allies finally realised that they must respond in kind, and the size of active armies rose to unprecedented levels. Napoleon's invasion force of Russia was 600,000; the battle of Leipzig in 1813 (the 'Battle of Nations') was the biggest battle of the nineteenth century. This battle, sometimes described as the birth of modern war, lasted for three days and was contested by 360,000 Russian, Austrian and Prussian troops against a French force of 200,000. The mass use of artillery was a portent of future wars, with the French gunners firing 200,000 shot and shells and the allies even more. Another feature of modern warfare was the huge casualty rate; mass armies ranged against each other produce mass casualties. The French forces suffered 73,000 casualties in the three days, the allies 54,000. Across the near quarter century of the French Wars an estimated four million Europeans had been killed with a substantial proportion of them civilians. Mercifully one of the limiting factors on the scale of battlefield losses was the undeveloped nature of the largely eighteenth-century weapons which were still used.

b) Economic Warfare

i) The Cost of War

One of the major constraints on warmakers in the eighteenth century, and on the size of their armies, was the sheer cost of raising, arming, feeding and replacing their fighting forces. As we have seen, the armies of the revolution and Napoleon smashed the limits on army size and the level of military activity. To achieve this there had to be a corresponding transformation in the funding of war. For the leaders of the revolution and Napoleon the answer was simple – the enemy would pay. This process had been set in motion by 1794 when the mass armies raised to defend the revolution could no longer be sustained by French resources and were sent abroad, almost anywhere, to live off foreign conquests. For the revolutionary armies this was a brutal and haphazard regime of forced requisition and theft, but under Napoleon it was elevated into a systematic, highly profitable funding mechanism. Apart from the continued requisition of

1814, English cartoonist George Cruikshank depicts Napoleon 'stripping other countries' assets to ward off the bankruptcy of the French exchequer'.

supplies, Napoleon's troops were motivated by the promise of booty; it was official burglary on an international scale. Indeed Napoleon himself did this on a grander level, stripping the finest art treasures from conquered territories, to be sent back to France as glittering evidence of the might of his empire. From 1805 onwards, with the defeat of each enemy power, he systematically extracted hundreds of millions of francs in contributions, taxes, tariffs and indemnities to shift the burden of war from France to the conquered territories. We must also take into account the sizeable contribution of troops from the defeated countries (which took a high priority in all of Napoleon's peace negotiations). War was not only a profitable business for Napoleon, it provided a lifeline for the entire empire. From 1805 onwards Napoleon's war profits contributed between 10 and 15 per cent of France's annual income. If for no other reason than the provision of state funds, Napoleon was shackled to a treadmill of perpetual war. To be set against the profits of war for the empire there were also significant losses. The costly defeats in Spain and Russia were both military and economic disasters. Just as the profits of war had propped up the empire, so the losses of war were to undermine the very foundations of the regime.

ii) The Trade War

From the very outset of war the economic power of Britain was used against the revolutionary forces. Britain was able to fight the war at arm's length by subsidising continental allies and keeping them in the conflict. But it was the trade war that was to have the greater impact and this was to be decided at sea. By 1799 the entire French merchant fleet had been swept from the sea and France was dependent on American and neutral ships to carry their exports. But it was after the British defeat of the French navy at Trafalgar in 1805, and Napoleon's victories against his main continental adversaries in 1805–7, that the trade war assumed greater importance. For Britain Napoleon's restrictive 'continental system' led to the loss of most of her European export markets, with resulting hardship and unrest at home. It also led directly to war with the USA in 1812 as Britain increasingly monitored and restricted the neutral's trade with Napoleonic Europe. But for Napoleon Britain's blockade led to nothing less than the unravelling of his entire empire. The regime was denied the financial contribution of international trade, and to make his blocking of British goods work he had to extend his continental system ever further, to Spain, Portugal, Italy, Sweden and Russia. Denied British imports, the great trading ports, and their dependent industries, of the North Sea, the Baltic and the Mediterranean, were ruined. The restrictions on British and colonial goods, and heavy-handed Napoleonic controls, produced a backlash in Spain and Russia and simmering resentment across most of Europe, including France. This discontent fuelled the patriotic uprising in Spain, as well as Russia's withdrawal from the continental system that provoked Napoleon's disastrous invasion. The trade war was a pointer to the future; warfare had now graduated into a struggle not just between armies, but also between competing economies and populations. It was another step towards total war.

c) Morale, Public Opinion and the Propaganda War

Another departure from the limited wars of the eighteenth century was the greater importance attached to the shaping of public opinion. Until the revolution the kings had paid little regard to public opinion. Wars were limited and short, armies were small and not representative of society, and the function of armies was to carry out the king's bidding, not the wishes of the people or the nation. The French revolution was to change all this. The revolution not only had to raise a mass army, it had to mobilise an entire nation to preserve the ideals of the revolution. The unprecedented level of participation and sacrifice required could only be achieved with the aid of a relentless propaganda campaign. Political pamphlets, cartoons, speeches, poems and songs rained down on the revolutionary citizens who were portrayed as leading a crusade for the universal rights of mankind against the 'reactionary tyrants'. In 1794 alone political commissars delivered 7.5 million pamphlets and 100,000 'republican songbooks' to French troops. The *levée en masse* was as much an ideological mobilisation as a military one. The old dynastic regimes countered by presenting themselves as the defenders of law, property and God-given order against the godless, murderous, republican hordes. Implicit in this exaggerated intensity of the struggle was the acceptance of unlimited war in terms of the complete overthrow of the enemy system. No longer was war fought for a slice of territory or trading concessions. It was now fought for a goal more often associated with the twentieth century: the complete destruction of one's enemy and the replacement of their government and society with one more acceptable to the victor.

As the war progressed motivations for the war effort began to change for both sides, and this is reflected in the propaganda. In France, as the revolution was replaced by Napoleon's military dictatorship, so for the fighting forces revolutionary zeal gave way to the rewards of loot and self-advancement. Under Napoleon, revolutionary appeals were suppressed and the emphasis shifted to the defence of the country, the glories of the empire, and increasingly the glories of the emperor. Napoleon was a master in the art of self-promotion but even he could not prevent the steady erosion of his support at home that was to play a major part in his downfall. After defeat in Russia in 1812 the Napoleonic spell was broken, the aura of invincibility was shattered, conscription requirements rose dramatically, and the economic hardships were felt more keenly. As Count Pasquier recorded at the time: 'A general anxiety prevailed ... There was no faith in anything any more, and every illusion had vanished.'[4]

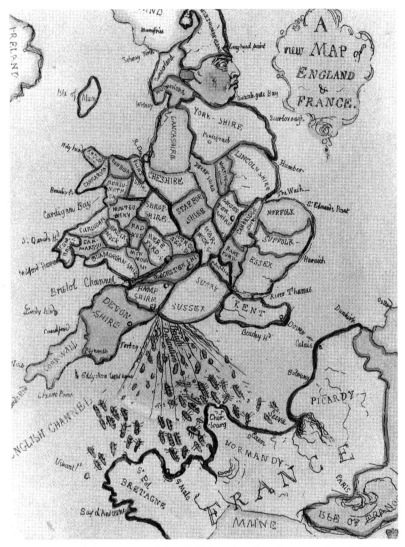

'The French Invasion; or John Bull, bombarding the Bum-Boats' 1793.
English cartoonist James Gillray portrays George III as the personification of
the nation 'repelling' the French invaders.

For the allies, the shift in the emphasis in propaganda was equally
significant. Increasingly appeals to the defence of the king and his
realm were replaced by new appeals to patriotism and common sacrifice for one's country. In Britain the reviled George III was rescued

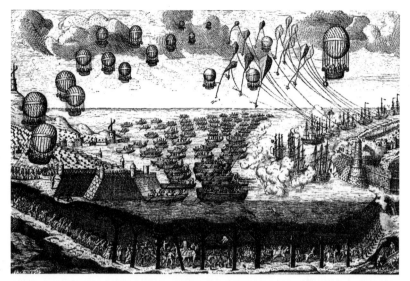

The proposed French invasion of Britain, 1803–5, as portrayed by a French cartoonist. The impressive invasion force is shown arriving by air, sea and underwater Channel tunnel.

'French volunteers marching to the conquest of Great Britain'. A less than impressed British cartoonist downplays the threat of invasion by depicting Napoleons' army as a ragbag of the sick, the feeble, and the enforced.

from his unpopularity by being cast as the epitome of the nation (see Gillray's cartoon on page 40). By 1805 Nelson's signal flags carried the nationalistic, rather than the royal, message: 'England expects that every man will do his duty.' In fighting the Napoleonic challenge a profound change was under way, identification with the king gave way to identification with the nation.

8 The Response of the Kings

> **KEY ISSUE** What were the varying ways in which the dynastic states attempted to meet the Napoleonic challenge?

Just as the revolutionary armies owed much of their success to the inadequacy and lack of unity amongst their opponents, so Napoleon was equally as fortunate. His long series of historic victories against Austria, Prussia and Russia up to 1807 were achieved against enemies who had fought separately and clung to the outdated practices of eighteenth-century warfare. Against such opponents Clausewitz was correct in asserting that Napoleon simply could not lose. The allies had tried appeasement and accommodation towards the aggressor, but were soon made aware of the massive financial cost and humiliation of this course of action. One by one they realised that Napoleon had to be overthrown, but to achieve this would require a transformation of their entire military organisation. Many changed their tactics, but more importantly they had to match the French numbers. Some, like Prussia, accepted that this would also entail radical social changes but believed it was a price worth paying. To defeat Napoleon the allies would have to become more like the French.

a) Prussia

Prussia's crushing defeat at Jena-Auerstadt in 1806 shook the kingdom out of its eighteenth-century complacency. By 1815 it had done more than any other ally to transform its military and its society to confront the challenge of Napoleon. In the wake of defeat King Frederick William III dismissed his elderly generals and appointed a younger generation of reforming officers (Scharnhorst, Gneisenau and Clausewitz) to remodel the Prussian army along French lines. The Prussians established a co-ordinated General Staff and adopted the French corps and division, their attack columns, their mass batteries of artillery, and light infantry skirmishers. Crucially the Prussian reformers managed to persuade their reluctant monarch to introduce mass conscription, a humane discipline system and the opening of officer status to all on the basis of ability. After Napoleon's defeat in Russia, a national revolt was declared against France and the king was forced to sanction conscription without exemptions. Unlike the resistance in Spain, which was civilian-based, the Prussian effort was state-led and directed through a much improved regular army. The army rose from 66,000 to 300,000 by 1813, in time to play a leading part in the decisive battles against Napoleon. The French invasions had provoked a Prussian Nation-in-Arms and a burning national ambition that would be a major factor in European history for over a century.

b) Austria

Austria was similarly galvanised by the comprehensive defeats of 1805 at Ulm and Austerlitz. The Austrians, under the guidance of the emperor's brother Charles, also adopted the new French tactics and organisation of war. These reforms ushered in the use of skirmishers, attack columns, mass artillery batteries, heavy attack cavalry, mobile corps and divisions, with reduced baggage trains and supplies based on requisition. However, there were areas where Austria's conservative reformers feared to tread; their leaders were determined to avoid the destabilising effect of mass conscription, and in a multi-national empire they dare not raise patriotic emotions. Despite this reluctance Archduke Charles was able to create a vast reserve militia from 1808, which could supply an additional 180,000 trained men when required. Napoleon's forces soon felt the effect of these reforms with their defeat at Aspern and their narrow victory at Wagram, both in 1809.

c) Russia

Russia, and its army, was the most backward of the great powers to be confronted by the challenge of Napoleon. Her conservatism was so culturally entrenched that she could not contemplate the conscription reforms undertaken by the French, or the Prussians after 1808. The most that the Russians did was to increase enlistment slightly and reduce the length of service for the serf-soldier from life to 25 years. Some reforms were made, such as the increase in skirmishers, the adoption of the corps system, and the huge Russian artillery was re-equipped. But the strength of the Russian army remained its size and the dogged determination of its troops, who were prepared to accept higher losses, and more brutal discipline, than any other European army. These strengths were most evident in the defence of Russia in 1812 when her army and her ancient society, inspired by the church, united in patriotic fury to decimate Napoleon's huge invasion force.

d) Britain

The most remarkable feature of the British army at the beginning of the French Wars was its size. The British parliament, ever suspicious of a standing army and resentful of its cost, had reduced the army to

40,000 men, the majority of whom were scattered around the furthest reaches of the empire. In the early months of the conflict Britain did what she normally did in time of war: she recruited from abroad. In 1793 the British army in Flanders consisted of 17,000 German troops and only 6,500 British. Although the numbers rose significantly as the war progressed, reaching 200,000 in 1809, most of these men served, and died, in the colonies. Britain steadfastly refused to adopt general conscription and retained the pattern of a small British field army, supplemented by foreign troops, throughout the conflict. Even at Waterloo only half of Wellington's army was British.

Despite the small size, and the eighteenth-century nature of the British army, it was surprisingly effective. Officers and men had won hard-earned experience in Portugal and Spain. Unlike the mass, untrained French army, the British army was a well-drilled, resolute, professional force that displayed the best qualities of eighteenth-century warfare. Also in Wellington they had a commander who was a master of established defensive tactics. Of all of the traditional powers Britain did least to emulate Napoleonic tactics and organisation because they alone had avoided the type of crushing defeat that had provoked the radical overhaul undertaken by her continental allies. The British infantry met the challenge of the French attack columns by reducing their three-deep line of fire to a broader, more effective, two lines, which actually delivered greater firepower. Even with a small army Britain proved to be the longest and arguably the most effective of Napoleon's adversaries. With Portuguese and Spanish support, Britain was able to tie down 300,000 of Napoleon's best troops in the Iberian campaign; her naval supremacy strangled French trade and provoked Napoleon into his destructive continental system. Also British wealth and burgeoning industry were able to provide the huge subsidies and mass-produced weapons to keep her continental allies in the struggle. The war had cost Britain three to four times the amount it cost France (partly because France was able to make her satellites and conquered territories foot the bill). But crucially it was a cost which Britain alone could afford.

9 Leadership

> **KEY ISSUE** What were the strengths and weaknesses of Napoleon as a military commander?

Napoleon's reputation as a military commander is still a matter of great debate. With an estimated 200,000 books and articles devoted to him there is an almost infinite range of opinion to choose from. For many historians he is the greatest military leader since Alexander the Great. Clausewitz actually described him as 'the God of War'. For others, such as Owen Connelly and Correlli Barnett, he 'blundered to glory'.[5] Many of his strengths and weaknesses have already been referred to in this chapter but it is worthwhile summarising the major points.

a) Strengths

- Unity of command. Napoleon was sole military and political leader of his nation. He could direct the full social and economic resources of his empire towards the war effort.
- His detailed planning of a battle was masterful.
- He successfully implemented the most effective military theories and practices. This led to the mobile corps system, the concentration of artillery on the weakest point, and the mixed order of infantry.
- The sweep, speed and scale of his operations, in an age of primitive communications, was awe-inspiring.
- His insistence on attack and the pursuit of the 'decisive battle' smashed the limited, defensive tactics of his eighteenth-century style opponents.
- His personal impact on morale was inspirational to his own side and dispiriting to his adversaries. Wellington claimed his appearance on the battlefield was worth 40,000 men. Napoleon deliberately crafted a personal bond with his troops.
- He was prepared to take risks and was a great improviser on the battlefield, which proved highly effective against rigid traditional opponents.
- For most of his wars Napoleon had the great numerical advantage of the Nation-in-Arms, and he was ruthless enough to use those numbers. He made the grim boast that he could afford 30,000 casualties a month.

b) Weaknesses/Criticisms

- Napoleon would not delegate command. Subordinate officers gained neither experience nor confidence. His vision, his health or his luck decided the outcome of battles.
- Napoleon's victories owe more to the incompetence and divisions among the allies than his own abilities.
- As the war continued the allies were able to copy his tactics and size of army and defeat him at his own game. His superiority, based upon larger numbers, was short-lived.
- Napoleon became trapped in a destructive cycle of continuous warfare. Only military conquests would prop up his empire and his army, but continuous war eroded his resources, his support and his manpower.
- His invasion of Russia was a disaster from which he and his armies could not recover. It was a direct result of Napoleon's bad cam-

paign planning, hopelessly inadequate supply arrangements and over-confidence.

- The 'Spanish ulcer' claimed 600,000 French lives and much needed resources but the war in Spain did not need to be fought. Napoleon could have personally led a heavier campaign to finish off resistance, or British goods could more easily have been blocked in the Pyrenees.
- Some writers have claimed that Napoleon fought some of his bloodiest campaigns primarily for pride and personal glory. As he admitted, 'In war men are nothing, one man is everything. What are a million men compared to a man such as I?'
- Napoleon could not limit his ambitions. His empire was over-stretched, extending beyond the control of his military machine and his personal supervision.
- Napoleon's repeated humiliating defeats on his opponents, and ruthless exploitation thereafter, provoked a patriotic backlash against France and a determination to reform and improve for renewed struggle.
- He was incapable of reaching a long-term political settlement or accepting a compromise peace. Decisive victories on the battle-field were not matched by a lasting diplomatic solution.
- Once the allies were united and reorganised Napoleon could not hope to match their combined resources and manpower.

10 Conclusion

> **KEY ISSUE** What were the areas of change and continuity in the wars of the French Revolution and Napoleon?

After the restraints and limitations of warfare in the eighteenth century the revolutionary and Napoleonic period represented a fundamental departure in the conduct and organisation of war. There were changes to tactics and strategy, the organisation and size of armies, and even the purpose of war. At the core of these changes was the radical transformation of the social and economic order of a major power to raise and sustain an army of revolutionary size. The sheer size of this force made change necessary in tactics, supplies and organisation and opened up new possibilities in warfare.

Napoleon inherited and perfected these changes and swept all before him as a result. His opponents, clinging to the social and military certainties of the eighteenth century, could not meet the French challenge without the reshaping of their own societies. They attempted individual resistance, half-hearted alliances and appeasement before reluctantly accepting that they must overhaul their outdated military, even if it opened the door to social and cultural changes. The wars also revealed many of the characteristics of modern warfare both on the battlefield and away from it in terms of a total war effort that included an economic war of attrition and the mobilisation of public opinion. But it is important to be aware of those enduring physical and technological restraints on warfare that prevent us from classifying the wars of this period as truly modern. It was to be the technological innovations of the industrial age that broke through those restraints and finally delivered the era of modern warfare.

References

1 G. Best, *War and Society in Revolutionary Europe* (Sutton, 1998), p. 63.
2 *Ibid.*, p. 92.
3 T.C.W. Blanning, *The Origins of the French Revolutionary Wars* (Longman, 1986), p. 164.
4 C. J. Esdaile, *The Wars of Napoleon* (Longman, 1995), p. 277.
5 O. Connelly, *Blundering to Glory* (Scholarly Resources, 1988).

Summary Diagram
Change and Continuity in the Nature of Warfare

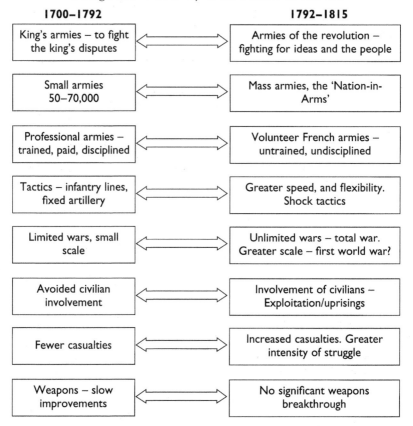

Answering essay questions on Chapter 3

As we have seen in the preceding chapter this period represents a significant advance in many areas of warfare. Its importance is reflected in the frequency with which questions are set on the topic. Because of the unique reputation of Napoleon most questions relate to his contribution and impact, but do not make the mistake of concentrating your efforts solely on him. Remember the significance of the revolutionary period before Napoleon's takeover and the response of the allies to the Napoleonic challenge. Some typical questions are:

1. How far is it true to say that the Revolutionary and Napoleonic Wars represent the birth of modern warfare?
2. How far do the Napoleonic Wars change the nature of warfare?
3. Does Napoleon deserve his reputation as the greatest military commander since Alexander the Great?
4. How far is it true to say that Napoleon's defeat in Russia was responsible for his downfall?

In considering the first question we are helped by the opening words of the title 'How far is it true to say' as this is asking us for both sides of the argument. For the sake of clarity, give all of one side of the argument, and then provide the other side.

Those features that support the idea of the wars as the birth of modern warfare could include: the scale of the wars, mass armies and mass casualties, the greater involvement of the civilian, the economic war of attrition, Napoleon's unlimited war aims, a total war effort requiring a Nation-in-Arms, and a propaganda war.

Those features which can be set against this argument include: primitive transport, eighteenth-century weapons, supplies were no longer guaranteed forcing armies to return to forage, and the limited nature of battles i.e. they were brief, usually one day and they covered a small area within the sight and control of one commander.

Question 2 requires a comparative approach with the last period of warfare, Dynastic Warfare 1700–1789, and therefore your information must be drawn from Chapters Two and Three. Examine the major characteristics of warfare, i.e. the nature of armies, tactics, weaponry, supplies etc. to make direct comparisons between the two periods. Remember there will be some elements that change as well as those that remain constant: you must point out each.

Question 3 is inviting a debate as there has been so much written on both sides of the argument. You may have a definite opinion on one side or the other but you are expected to provide a survey of the major points on both sides. Present one side of the argument first before presenting the counter argument. Remember to refer to some leading authors who have made a contribution to the debate; short memorable quotes (in the right context!) make a good impression.

Essay 4 asks you to assess the relative importance of one of the factors responsible for Napoleon's downfall. Start off with an examination of the Russian campaign and its place in Napoleon's collapse and then point out some of the other relevant causes that have to be taken into account. These could include the 'Spanish ulcer', economic pressures, the loss of support at home, the decline of the French forces, the revived strength of his enemies etc.

Source-based questions on Chapter 3

Read the extracts from the *levée en masse* on page 27, and from Clausewitz on page 28.

a) What does Clausewitz mean by 'suddenly war again became the business of the people' (page 28, lines 1–2)? *(10 marks)*

b) Why has the *levée en masse* been described as a prescription for total war? *(10 marks)*

c) What were the motivations for 'the people' to comply with the *levée*? *(10 marks)*

d) Using both sources, and your own knowledge, explain how the events described here, and their consequences, represent a turning point in the nature of warfare. *(20 marks)*

History exams at just about every level now contain source-based or document questions. These sources will either be 'primary' (first hand, contemporary), or 'secondary' (produced after the event, usually a historian's account). The majority of sources you will be presented with are primary.

1. Pay particular attention to the exact wording of the question. Your answers need to be direct, relevant and without excessive description. The most common failing in these types of question is for students to use the sources as a loose starting point for a discursive, essay-type response. Refer directly to the source (giving the line number), to illustrate the point you are making.

2. You will always be given a line or two that tells you about the source (the 'accreditation'). This is a very important part of the source: it will give you essential information such as who it is by, to whom it is directed, the date, and often where it was produced or recorded. Bear this information in mind as you read the source as it will usually 'open up' the document. For example:

i) Who is it by? What do we know about this person, what expectation might we have of his or her views? In this case one of the authors is Clausewitz, who was a military writer and reformer very impressed by the changes brought in by the revolutionaries' method of war. How is this revealed in what he says or the language that he uses?

ii) To whom is it directed? This is a basic, but often revealing question. In the case of the *levée en masse* the decree is directed towards the whole nation and describes the role that each section will play. Again the language used is revealing; it is emotive and used to produce a passionate response – it is rhetoric. After reading the chapter you will be able to answer how far the reality matched the rhetoric, and for how long.

iii) When was the source produced? Think very carefully about the date of the source, as it will place the document/event in its precise historical context.

iv) What is being said and why? This is probably the most important question to ask of a document; what was the motive or purpose of the originator of the source? For the originators of the *levée* the purpose was to exhort people to action, but it was also an instruction, on pain of death, for all to take part in the war effort. Remember that you should not automatically accept the truthfulness (reliability) of the source: it might be unintentionally or deliberately biased or propagandist.

Use these basic questions as a quick checklist on any source and bring in your wider knowledge of the period to place the source in historical context.

4 War in the Industrial Age 1815–1914

POINTS TO CONSIDER

This chapter begins with the attempt of the kings to revert to the military securities of the eighteenth century. It then traces the increasingly significant impact of industrialisation on the nature of warfare in the wars of the nineteenth century in Europe. Note the changes in warfare brought about by industrialisation in terms of weaponry, size of armies, transport and the increasing significance of public opinion.

KEY DATES

1815	Overthrow of Napoleon and return to traditional armies.
1848–9	Suppression of liberal revolutions by royal armies.
1854–6	The Crimean War: Britain and France against Russia.
1859	The Franco-Austrian War to secure Italian unification.
1860–65	The United States Civil War.
1864–71	The wars of German unification (against: Denmark, Austria, and France).
1877–8	Russian-Turkish War.
1899–1902	The Boer War: Boer uprising against British rule in South Africa.
1904–5	Russian-Japanese War.
1914	Outbreak of World War One.

1 The Role and Composition of Armies after the Fall of Napoleon

KEY ISSUE How did the kings try to return their armies to their traditional role?

a) The Attempt to Turn Back the Clock

The influence of Napoleon did not end with his defeat and exile in 1815, nor even with his death in 1821. The forces he had helped to unleash – nationalism, liberalism and militarism – were to play a leading role in the ensuing century. The dynastic states that had survived the revolution and Napoleon, however, wanted to hold back or reverse these subversive trends and attempted to return to the social, political and military securities of the eighteenth century. Across Europe there was an attempt to turn back the military clock to the eighteenth century, with smaller professional armies consisting of long-term troops and aristocratic officers. This was most urgent in

France. The restored Bourbon monarchy, fearing the democratising and disruptive effect of conscription, abolished the practice. They removed Napoleonic officers and returned to the earlier practice of appointing more reliable foreign troops and officers. In Prussia, the country most transformed by the struggle against Napoleon, the king now turned against the army reformers who had saved his throne, sidelining them and allowing the steady dilution of their reforms. In Russia and Austria reforms were abolished and their armies reverted to being agents of national and social repression. Britain alone had avoided invasion and the modernising contamination of Napoleon; her victory and imperial dominance allowed military complacency. Reforms were considered unnecessary and the purchase of officer commissions continued unchecked. Both parliament and people were exhausted by a quarter century's military burden and reverted to their more traditional small colonial army filled with social misfits and foreign mercenaries.

b) The Army's Policing Role

It was not just the size and composition of armies which changed in the decades following the overthrow of Napoleon. During the quarter century of the French Wars, armies had represented ideas and causes such as liberty or national defence. After the defeat of Napoleon these dangerous notions could not be allowed to continue; the armies were depoliticised. Armies were no longer to represent the nation and the people, they were to return to their eighteenth-century function of preserving the power and authority of the king, usually against the demands of his people. Following the Congress of Vienna of 1815, a remarkable stability in European affairs kept the peace for 40 years and the armies of Europe were used far more against their own people than they were in fighting other armies. In the multi-national empires of Russia and Austria national and racial suppression was the primary military concern, and even in France the army proved as reliable a conservative force as any other major European army. In an age before modern police forces, army units were garrisoned in towns not so much for their defence but for the control of the civilian populace and the heavy-handed suppression of unlawful or radical activities. In Britain this gave rise to the Peterloo massacre in Manchester in 1819 where mounted troops rode into a large crowd assembled to hear radical speakers. Ten people were killed and several hundred injured. For liberals and radicals like Percy Bysshe Shelley in his poem 'Queen Mab' the use of the army for this purpose was an outrage and the troops were no better than 'hired assassins'.

> 'These are the hired bravos who defend the tyrant's throne – the bullies of his fear.'[1]

The true value of the armies as the defenders of the autocratic monarchies was revealed in 1848 after a wave of liberal and national revolutions in the capital cities of continental Europe. The revolutions were essentially urban affairs and, after early successes, they were rolled back by the kings and their large, reliable peasant armies. The packing of armies with an obedient, non-political peasantry had been a deliberate long-term policy. The peasantry was by far the largest class in nineteenth-century Europe, especially in the eastern empires, but their most valuable characteristic for their rulers was their indifference to liberalism and nationalism and their loathing of revolution. Peasant conservatism was the backbone of continental armies until diluted by urbanisation and the mass conscription of the 1890s.

2 Industrialisation and Weapons Technology 1815–1854

> **KEY ISSUE** What were the major developments in military and non-military technology?

Owing to the impact of the industrial revolution, the nineteenth century saw some of the greatest changes in human history. Industrialisation with its factory system involved mass production, improved technology and more effective communications. At a wider level it produced a more organised, more urbanised population and supported an increase in the size of populations. All of these changes facilitated a substantial increase in the power, size and destructiveness of armies.

a) The Rifle

The greatest change in weapons technology in the first half of the century was a series of interconnected developments that led to the modern infantry rifle.

i) The percussion cap. More reliable firing was provided by the introduction of the percussion cap using the recently discovered fulminate of mercury, an explosive that detonated once struck. This sealed cap virtually eliminated the 20 per cent misfires of the previous flintlock muskets due to damp or wind, thereby increasing infantry firepower. The British army adopted the percussion cap in 1839 and it proved its worth in the Crimean War.

ii) The Minie Bullet. Rifled muskets had been used in European armies since the eighteenth century. Their main drawback was the difficulty of forcing the musket ball down the barrel of the gun against the rifle grooves, and the length of time this took. In 1849 the French Minie bullet overcame this problem as it could be easily dropped down the barrel of the rifle but would expand on firing to fit the rifled grooves. The effect was dramatic: the new Minie rifle had an accurate range of 600 yards, up to five times as far as the smoothbores. They were also cheaper to produce than previous rifles and could be fitted with a bayonet.

iii) The Dreyse rifle. In the 1840s a Prussian engineer, Dreyse, developed another significant breakthrough by inventing the breech-loading rifle. The bullet was slotted into a chamber, ready for firing, at the base of the barrel. The Dreyse 'needle rifle' had two major advantages. Firstly, it could load and fire four or five times more quickly than a muzzle-loader. Secondly, a breech-loading rifle, unlike the muzzle-loader, could be loaded and fired from a lying position, thereby allowing its user, for the first time, to take effective cover. Early technical difficulties held up the wider adoption of the Dreyse breech-loader until it was demonstrated to devastating effect in the Prussian-Austrian war of 1866.

These developments represent the coming of age of the rifle. They were now faster-loading, more reliable, and had greater range and accuracy; they were by far the most destructive weapons ever placed in the hands of the infantry. The implications for tactics were profound: the enhanced range and firepower of the rifle transferred the tactical advantage to the defender, especially if the soldiers used the added protection of trenches.

b) Artillery

The technological breakthroughs of rifling and breech-loading in small arms could also theoretically be applied to the artillery. But the development of artillery generally did not keep up with the progress in infantry rifles until the late 1860s. In 1845 a breech-loading, rifled, artillery gun was invented, though no country would face the cost of re-equipment. But in the Crimean War a number of British smooth-bore cannon were converted into a simplified rifled form and immediately displayed their greater range and accuracy in the bombardment of Sebastopol. Following this proof in action, all the major powers began to develop breech-loading, rifled artillery.

c) Non-Military Technology

i) Railways

The greatest advance in military capability did not arise from weapons innovation but from the revolution in transport and communications. The transport revolution was based upon the development of the steam engine in the early nineteenth century that powered rail transport and the steamboat. The steamboat transformed trans-oceanic warfare and extended European power over non-Europeans; railways transformed warfare across the developed continents of North

America and Western Europe. Previously an army could only move as fast as a fully laden man could march. His supplies, drawn by horse and wagon, could only be guaranteed up to a range of 70 miles. By the 1840s the train transport of troops and supplies smashed through these restrictions of time and space. In 1848 the conservative monarchs used the railways to transport reliable troops to their capitals to reclaim their authority from the revolutionaries. The wars of the mid-century were the first to demonstrate the revolutionary impact of the railways. Once carefully integrated into the war effort, the railway represented the greatest change in the strategy of war until superseded by motor and air transport.

Railways expanded military capability in terms of:

- the speed of delivering armies
- the ability to deliver a greater numbers of troops
- the means to keep those forces supplied
- the fighting ability of the troops, as they had not been exhausted by long marches to the battlefield
- the health and well-being of armies at the front, as the sick and wounded could be quickly removed and fresh troops supplied.

As the implications of the revolution in transport were understood it became clear that its greatest impact would be on the size of armies. Theoretically the size of an army now depended on the number of available men in a country and the whole country's efforts to supply them. Armies expanded massively on all sides: hundreds of thousands or millions of men could now be delivered quickly and efficiently to their fate on the battlefield.

ii) The Electric Telegraph

The first half of the nineteenth century also saw the invention, and use for military purposes, of the telegraph. This allowed for the instantaneous sending of messages over hundreds of miles between political leaders, commanders and their armies. The range of military command and political interference had been expanded dramatically. Yet on the battlefield the fighting forces still had to use 'runners' for written messages, or communicated by drums, bugles and flags. Newspapers were quick to take advantage of the telegraph to provide up-to-date coverage of battles and campaigns, which brought the public gaze on to the war effort and increased the public's identification with the army. This was most famously demonstrated in the Crimean War, where reporters were able to make use of a specially laid undersea telegraph linked up to the main European network. Army commanders now had the dubious privilege of having their successes and failures subject to immediate public and political scrutiny. As the commander of the British forces in the Crimea complained, 'the confounded telegraph has ruined everything'.[2] Cheap newspapers and a wider readership were also products of the industrial age and through them domestic public opinion was brought into the calculations of strategy, often overriding purely military considerations.

3 The Crimean War 1854–6

> **KEY ISSUE** What was the technological difference between the two sides and what impact did this have on tactics and casualties?

The Crimean War is the first of a series of wars in the mid-century between the great powers in which many of the features of modern warfare begin to emerge. This survey of the wars concentrates on the impact of industrialisation on warfare and the efforts of strategists to come to terms with the new realities of combat.

a) British and French Technological Lead

The Crimean War was fought by France, Britain, Turkey and Austria against Russian expansion into South-East Europe. It was a limited, amphibious war that displayed both old and new features. As the first major war in Europe for 40 years, it acted as a showcase for new weapons which were studied and adopted by the major European armies. In contrast to this, the tactical lessons of the war were not so readily absorbed. At sea the French navy demonstrated the absolute superiority of ironclad ships and explosive shells against unprotected wooden vessels. On land both the British and French forces demonstrated the greater range and power of rifled artillery and their infantry was equipped with the latest percussion rifles. The British and French forces also had a telling technological lead in terms of transport and logistics which enabled them to transfer large quantities of weapons, supplies and troops to the Crimea in less than three weeks by steamship. British engineers also built the first tactical military railway, a 25-mile track linking Balaclava harbour to the British trenches, which delivered an unheard-of 240 tons of food and supplies each day.

Despite these technological advantages the allies did not overwhelm their Russian adversaries. Partly this was due to allied shortcomings in leadership and organisation, with the British especially lacking in these areas. Fortunately for Britain they were up against an even more incompetent opponent. Against allied rifle technology in both artillery and infantry the Russians produced no rifled land weapons. Russian inferiority in this department was final proof to all observers of the obsolescence of the smoothbore musket. Russian industrial backwardness was also seen in chaotic supplies, hopelessly inadequate levels of production and non-existent quality controls. Overall the Russians had an army in excess of 1 million men, but it was garrisoned throughout the empire and Russia did not have a railway system remotely capable of delivering these forces to the war zone. Their armies would have to march for months to reach the front. The Crimean War was beginning to reveal to Russia, and the wider world, the revolutionary impact of industrialisation on the balance of military power. Russia simply did not have the technological ability, in terms of weapons or logistics, to make use of their potential advantages in numbers and geography. Traditional military power was being superseded by that conferred by industrialisation.

b) Tactics

The Crimean War not only acted as a demonstration ground for new weapons it also provided valuable lessons in the evolution of tactics. The greatest change in land warfare was the substantial increase in the range, accuracy and firepower of percussion cap rifles and the rifled artillery. Faced with such weapons the Russian troops persisted in the Napoleonic column charge; but their frontal assaults could only hope to succeed against defenders equipped with old-style, slow-firing muskets with short range. Against defenders armed with the new rifles and more accurate artillery, firing explosive shrapnel shells, the attacking force stood no chance. Even the Russian forces with their inferior weapons proved the dominance of defensive fire if protected by trenches. It did not, however, prevent both sides from launching suicidal attacks against well-protected positions. Indeed the experience made little impact on attack-obsessed military thinkers for many decades to come. The legend of Napoleonic tactics was more powerful than modern weapons. What should have been another clear lesson, displayed in such striking fashion by the ill-fated charge of the Light Brigade, was the redundancy of the cavalry charge against modern artillery and infantry. It was, however, a lesson that took a long time to learn.

c) Casualties

Although the Crimean War was only a limited war, the casualty count was staggering. The Russians sustained nearly half a million casualties, the Turks up to 400,000, and the French and British together suffered 300,000 killed or wounded. This appears to be a portent of the industrialised slaughter to come, but it must be borne in mind that the losses reflect an earlier type of warfare in the fact that four-fifths of these casualties were caused by exposure, sickness, filthy sanitary conditions and totally inadequate medical facilities. In the new age of rapid newspaper coverage these disgraceful conditions became the focus of outraged British public opinion, leading to the resignation of a government and the dispatch of the redoubtable Florence Nightingale to establish improved, and hygienic, nursing care.

4 The Franco-Austrian War 1859

> **KEY ISSUE** How did the Franco-Austrian War reveal the strategic potential of railways?

Warfare in the next 12 years in Europe was dominated by the wars of Italian and German unification. The war of 1859, which resulted in partial Italian unification, provided a number of examples of the continuing modernisation of warfare.

a) Railways and Strategy

On the technological side, railways were used for the first time in warfare to mobilise and deploy the French armies. The different speeds of mobilisation of the two armies were clear for all to see. A French army of 120,000 was transported to Northern Italy by rail in less than two weeks, a distance that previously would have required a two-month march. In contrast the Austrian army marched across difficult ground to the battlefields at a speed often of only three miles per day. The French armies were also bolstered by the rapid deployment of another 70,000 troops delivered by steam-ship. The crucial advantage of arriving first on the battlefield in superior numbers, in peak condition and fully supplied, was the primary lesson offered to military observers. This does not mean that the new technology of rail and telegraph was seamlessly incorporated into the war effort. Telegraphs appeared to do no more than confuse both sides. The Austrian reserve force, when they finally managed to make use of railways, only succeeded in getting lost and missing the battle. The French armies may have been dispatched rapidly to the front but it was often the case that their guns and ammunition were left behind. Clearly more advanced means of communication could increase the range and scale of military operations, but it also demanded more sophisticated planning and co-ordination at the highest level.

b) Weapons and Tactics

In terms of weapons the French had a clear advantage in artillery with their new rifled cannon, the 'Napoleon', so much so that it virtually decided every battle in which it took part. With an accurate range of 3,500 yards it easily outfired the older Austrian smooth-bores with a range of only 2,000 yards. The French gunners could station their cannon beyond the range of the Austrian artillery and destroy them without coming under fire themselves. The French rifled cannon was the most successful, and subsequently, the most copied weapon of the war. The French infantry, despite their recent experience in the Crimea, reverted to Napoleonic shock columns making bayonet charges against the opposing infantry. This tactic against improved rifles should have proved as suicidal to the French as it had to the Russians five years previously. Yet the French troops were saved by the inability of the poorly trained, ill-educated Slav conscripts, who could barely use their new rifles nor even understand the orders of their Austrian commanders. Once again most military observers convinced themselves of the superiority of spirited attack over well-armed defence.

5 The Impact of Prussia: Wars of German Unification 1864–71

> **KEY ISSUES** What were the reasons for Prussian military supremacy during this period? What were the lessons drawn from these wars?

The wars of German Unification were the most influential wars of the nineteenth century after the fall of Napoleon. They were a dramatic series of wars fought in the heart of Europe between some of the leading great powers of the age. They seemed to deliver the holy grail of decisive victory in both military and political terms. None of the wars lasted for more than a year, and in reality they were all decided in one or two quick battles, yet they produced results that transformed the balance of power in Europe irrevocably.

a) Prussian Reforms

Prussia's victories were not the product of a temporary superiority, they were achieved as a result of long-term organisational reforms, meticulous strategic planning, and spectacular industrial growth.

i) The General Staff

The Prussian General Staff had been formed in the Napoleonic Wars to develop army doctrine and war plans, but it did not have direct control over officers in the field until Helmuth von Moltke became Chief of the General Staff from 1857 to 1888. Moltke, like other members of the General Staff, had been selected strictly on merit, and all were highly trained yet flexible and imaginative. Moltke transformed the Prussian General Staff into the most effective army leadership in Europe, using brilliant strategic planning and painstaking attention to detail. They were the only army leadership to practise war games; they studied past campaigns and spent years mapping the country for military purposes. With the increase in the size of armies, and their greater range and speed of movement made possible by the railways, the Prussians were the first to realise the necessity of this evolution of command. In the age of the telegraph Prussia had effectively taken the control of armies out of the hands of battlefield commanders and placed it in the hands of General Staff Headquarters.

ii) The Strategic Use of Railways

The General Staff not only recognised the military potential of railways, they sent their best strategic brains into the railway section to integrate rail and telegraph into the core of Prussian war planing. Moltke himself spent the 1840s in the army's railway section and advocated state spending on railways rather than fortresses. As he argued in 1843, 'Every new development of railways is a military advantage'.[3] Moltke saw that advantage grow significantly between 1850 and 1870 when Prussia's railtrack trebled as a result of sustained industrial growth, giving her a substantial lead over all her continental rivals. Moltke organised rail mobilisation exercises and integrated state and private railways into Prussia's military strategy so that (unlike in other countries) the army would have first call on their services when required. Owing to Prussia's strategic central position between powerful potential enemies, the co-ordinated use of railways was to have a more profound effect on Prussia's fate than any other nation.

iii) Conscription and the Prussian Nation-in-Arms

In the 1850s War Minister Roon expanded the Prussian army by extending conscription to all social classes, and their length of service was increased from two to three years in the regular army followed by four years in the reserve. This was at a time when most European armies were made up of a small number of long service regulars. The Prussian recruits were better educated and better trained, especially in marksmanship, than any other European army. By 1862 Prussia had doubled the size of the regular army and dramatically increased its budget in readiness for a bid for great power status.

iv) Prussian Tactics

The first country to feel the might of the Prussian Nation-in-Arms was Denmark in 1864. The Danes fell victim to two of the trademark features of the new Prussian way of war – faster mobilisation via their strategic railways and greater firepower from their Dreyse breech-loading rifle. During the course of the wars of unification Moltke formulated revolutionary tactics to best exploit the capabilities of the weapon. This was to lead to the legendary Prussian/German 'mission tactics' and represents the greatest tactical response to the enhanced firepower of defenders. Moltke concluded that the age of frontal attack was over; his tactics were to avoid frontal assault by adopting a more flexible, skirmishing movement, not just for some units but for all. Small units were to attack swiftly, outflanking the enemy and encircling them to finish them off in a 'ring of fire' (*Kesselschlacht*). Tactical decision making in the field was devolved down to the infantrymen. This mobile tactic was made possible by the more flexible capabilities of the Dreyse rifle and the highly trained Prussian soldier. It was to be the core of successful German infantry tactics for nearly a century.

b) The Defeat of Austria

By 1866 Moltke had further refined his mobilisation plans and tactics to achieve the most decisive victory of one great power over another since the days of Napoleon. The Prussians brilliantly followed Napoleonic patterns of strategic movement, now updated and improved by the use of railways and telegraph communication. The Prussian force of 250,000, delivered by five separate railway lines, was deployed across 300 miles and converged rapidly on the enemy positions. It was a nineteenth-century foretaste of Blitzkrieg. In contrast Austria's mobilisation was disorderly and slow, making little use of their own railway network. The main battle took place at Sadowa (also called Könnigratz). The Prussians, converging on the battlefield, avoided a frontal assault but, using mission tactics, broke up their forces into small, mobile units to swarm around the flanks of the enemy positions and blast them from all sides with the greater firepower of the Dreyse rifle. The other advantage of the Dreyse was its ability to be fired from a lying position against Austrian forces that were fully exposed. The effect was demoralising on Austria's half-hearted multi-national army, many of whom fled the battlefield. Sadowa represented a crushing defeat: the Austrians suffered 44,000 casualties to the Prussians' 9,000. The war had lasted a mere seven weeks and was decided by one major battle. Prussia had taken a further dramatic step towards the domination of Germany, increasing their population by 7,000,000, and, with contributions from other German states, raising their total army to 1 million.

c) The Defeat of France

The Franco-Prussian War of 1870–1 produced a Prussian victory no less dramatic and overwhelming than that achieved against Austria. Once again it displayed the Prussian brilliance in mobilisation, strategic movement, organisational leadership and firepower. Again equally as significant were the glaring weaknesses and incompetence of their adversary. Added to these advantages was an overwhelming numerical superiority for Prussia. On the eve of war the French army stood at 400,000 against the Prussian/German force of 1 million. The French mobilisation proved to be as chaotic as it had in 1854 and 1859: 'French mobilisation in short resembled a disturbed ants' nest', writes Brian Bond.[4] In contrast the German mobilisation was even faster than its electrifying performance in 1866.

The French forces had a genuine advantage in their new breech-loading rifle (the *Chassepot*), which had twice the range of the Prussian Dreyse. The French were also equipped with an early heavy machine gun, their 'wonder weapon' the *mitrailleuse*, which could fire up to 200 rounds a minute, but this had been kept so secret that hardly any French troops knew how to use it. The French therefore had potentially greater defensive firepower but poor leadership and organisation. Superior German artillery and tactics, and sheer weight of numbers, swept aside any possible French advantages. The new Prussian breech-loading, rifled steel cannon, supplied by steel makers Krupps, had a far greater range and accuracy than the French guns. From long range they could decimate the French artillery and infantry without themselves coming under fire. The war was effectively decided by two major battles: the siege of French forces at Metz and the encirclement of the relieving French armies, under the personal leadership of Napoleon III, at Sedan. Both battles were decided by the more mobile tactics and longer range artillery of the Prussians to blast the French into submission. At Sedan the entire army of 104,000 survivors, plus their emperor, capitulated to the enemy. This was a stunning victory for the modernised artillery; the Prussian infantry were barely needed. It signalled a turning point in the battlefield balance of power. The long dominance of the musket and rifle was being overtaken by the artillery.

d) Lessons Drawn from the Prussian Victories

Prussia's victory over France was even more momentous than its victory over Austria. In three very short and decisive wars Prussia had established itself, in the form of the German Empire, as the strongest military power Europe had ever witnessed. In the face of such staggering political and military results European strategists desperately sought the lessons of the Prussian revolution so that they might apply them to their own military establishment. Just as the enemies of Napoleon I in 1806 had accepted that, for their very survival, they must 'become more like the French', so the contemporaries of the newly united Germany realised, with some alarm, that they must 'become more like the Germans'.

The areas of German excellence, which were recognised and widely copied, were:

- The importance of rapid mobilisation facilitated by a railway system co-ordinated for military purposes
- The obsession with sweeping plans of attack
- The importance of a General Staff as the essential 'brain' of the army
- The acceptance of the expanded German 'Nation-in-Arms' based upon the mass conscription of short-term, highly trained conscripts supplemented by a huge pool of battle-ready reserves.

The consequences of these assumptions were dramatic: they plunged

The Battle of Sedan 1870. One of the first photographs of a battle in progress. Notice the Prussian troops in attacking formations in the background.

Europe into an increasingly frantic arms race, they led to the expansion of armies to almost insupportable levels, and they induced a widespread identification of the military with the nation that made national war more likely. So dazzled were Europeans by the Prussian successes that they concluded that it was the strength and speed of the Prussian attack, not the unpreparedness of the Austrian and French defenders, that explained this transformation in the balance of power. Thus the major conclusion drawn from the wars which most influenced military thinking and plans up to 1914 was of the importance of attack, its speed and its force. Yet closer examination of the battles of 1870 would have revealed that not one position was taken by frontal assault. It was these mistaken assumptions which helped prepare the way for the bloodbath of 1914.

6 Industry and War: Further Weapons Development

KEY ISSUE How did advances in weapons technology strengthen the power of the defensive?

a) The Rifle

The next step in the development of the modern rifle was the introduction of the magazine rifle into European armies from 1885 onwards. Previously infantrymen loaded one bullet at a time but rifles could now take up to nine bullets in their magazine (loading chamber), therefore reducing loading time so that trained soldiers could fire once every four seconds. With the development of metal-cased cartridges in the 1870s, and smokeless propellants (cordite) in the 1880s, riflemen could fire their repeating rifles without the usual cloud of smoke which obscured their aim and gave away their own position. Cartridges became smaller and men could now carry far more. In 1866 soldiers could only carry and use 60 rounds, by 1914 this had increased to 200. The firepower of the rifle had taken another massive step forward.

b) Artillery

By the 1860s most artillery guns were rifled, thereby increasing their range and accuracy. The next major step forward was the application of the new stronger steel technology to artillery. In 1870 the Prussian army demonstrated the battle-winning potential of their recently supplied Krupps steel breech-loading artillery. The steel cannons were lighter, therefore more mobile, and had a far greater range than their French adversaries. Once again European armies scrambled to follow the German lead. The power of artillery was further enhanced by the development of high explosives such as cordite, TNT and lyddite in the 1880s. The explosives left no cloud of gunsmoke to give away the gunners' position and, as the range of artillery expanded to five miles, they could fire safely from concealed positions often miles behind the front. In the Russo-Japanese war 1904-5 forward observers with field telephones guided artillery to its target. By 1914 heavy artillery had a range of more than 20 miles, and a few a range in excess of 50 miles! The rate of fire had been transformed by the development of recoilless cannon in the 1890s (which automatically returned the gun to its original firing position ready to fire again). Previously the gunners would have to push the gun back into place and resight the weapon before each firing, allowing only three or four rounds a minute. With recoilless guns the artillery approached 1914 with a rate of fire equal to that of the rifleman.

c) The Machine Gun

The introduction of new weapons was not simply a matter of technological innovation; the adoption of the machine gun also demonstrates how it was often determined by the prevailing political or cultural climate. The conservative military establishment accepted the progress in artillery and rifles as refinements to the long-standing, traditional weapons of cannon and musket. The development of the modern machine gun by Hiram Maxim, however, was a radical challenge to their accepted view of warfare. Unlike the earlier French *mitrailleuse* or U.S. Gatling gun, which were hand-cranked revolver cannons, Maxim's version was fully automatic, belt-fed and water-cooled, capable of firing 600 rounds a minute. It was a staggering advance on previous rates of fire. The one ton *mitrailleuse* had been used as an inferior artillery weapon, but the Maxim machine gun at a mere 40 pounds could be manually wheeled or carried to support the infantry. Yet despite the massive potential of the machine gun, the officer class throughout Europe resisted its adoption. Commanders and their officers clung to the belief that the raw courage of the individual, and the morale and discipline of their fighting forces, were more important than any advance in mass produced technology. The machine gun threatened to reduce war to an industrial process and remove the role of the individual.

However, in the struggle to acquire colonies in Africa and elsewhere, small European forces were often greatly outnumbered by native warriors and the machine gun was seen as a devastating replacement for troops. The one-sided victory of the British over the Sudanese at the battle of Omdurman in 1898 was a stark demonstration of the disparity between an industrialised army and a pre-indus-

The *Mitrailleuse* ('the grape-shot firer'): the French forerunner to the Maxim machine gun. Notice the multi-barrel design and the cartridge case manually slotted into place.

trial one. Using artillery, magazine rifles and 20 machine guns, the small British force unleashed a torrent of firepower killing 11,000 Sudanese for the loss of just 28 Britons. For many observers, even on the victorious side, there were unsettling implications. The young Winston Churchill, who had taken part in the battle, was fully aware of the depersonalisation of the conflict and commented that it had simply been 'a matter of machinery'. The machine gun made nonsense of numerical superiority and was a significant feature in the expansion of European power in Africa. As Hilaire Belloc wrote in his poem 'The Modern Traveller':

> 'Whatever happens, we have got
> The Maxim gun, and they have not.'[5]

For two decades the machine gun became associated with colonial operations and the routing of 'backward natives', and as such it was regarded as having little relevance to the European situation. The Russo-Japanese war 1904–5, however, provided a bloody demonstration of the power of the machine gun. The German army then began to adopt machine guns; and in the tense atmosphere of the arms race the French quickly responded. The British, however, found further reasons to dismiss the relevance of the Russo-Japanese experience and entered the First World War woefully short of the gun and troops experienced in its operation.

7 Tactics and Strategy

> **KEY ISSUES** Why did commanders cling to the idea of the offensive? How was this reflected in their strategic plans and military build-up?

a) Tactics: The Cult of the Offensive

The nineteenth century, as a result of industrialisation, was characterised by a series of technological breakthroughs in weaponry and communications that transformed the nature of warfare. These innovations had the cumulative effect of increasing the range, the rate of fire, and the general destructiveness of modern weaponry. This effectively shifted the balance of power on the battlefield from the attacker to the defender. Yet, despite this, there remained a 'cultural lag' between the invention of these weapons and their acceptance and effective utilisation by the military establishment. The reputation of Napoleon and his insistence on attack still cast its spell over military commanders until deep into the latter part of the nineteenth century. His memory was kept alive in tactical terms by the leading military writer of the day, Antoine Jomini. The Napoleonic legacy perpetuated the 'cult of the offensive' which saw the frontal attack attempted in most of the wars of the nineteenth century despite the ever increasing firepower of the defender.

Technology was creating an ever wider fire zone, or 'no-man's-land', in which exposed troops could not expect to survive. Yet despite the mounting evidence many commanders still adhered to the older belief in cavalry and infantry attack. The failure of these attacks in recent conflicts was dismissed as a failure of morale, organisation, or numbers. The French army command was especially obsessed with the 'offensive spirit' between 1871 and 1914. As late as 1912 General Joffre, Chief of the French General Staff, stated: 'The French army, returning to its traditions, no longer knows any other law than that of the attack. All attacks are to be pushed to the limit, with firm determination to charge the enemy with the bayonet, in order to destroy him'.[6] It was this suicidal faith in the spirit of the French forces against modern weaponry that saw sections of the French army, wearing red pantaloons, blue tunics and no helmets, make disastrous frontal attacks on the German army in 1914. The British army, despite its more recent experience in the Boer War 1899–1902 (where at least it adopted camouflage khaki uniforms), was equally outdated. The British cavalry training manual of 1907 instructed its readers: 'It must be accepted as a principle that the rifle, effective as it is, cannot replace the effect produced by the speed of the horse, the magnetism of the charge, and the terror of cold steel.' In an age before reliable motorised transport, cavalry did have a role to play in reconnaissance but the days of the cavalry charge were, or should have been, over. Despite this, under the influence of Generals French and Haig, in 1909 the lance was reintroduced into the British cavalry and remained in service for another 20 years.

b) Strategic Plans and the Numbers Game

The military and political leaders of Europe therefore approached 1914 with a set of dangerous assumptions and misunderstandings. It was universally believed a major war was very likely, if not inevitable, and that the war, following the example of Prussia's wars, would be short and winnable. Given the numbers involved, the massive economic consequences, and the potential loss of life, no one could imagine the war continuing for more than a few months. It would be decided in a few weeks by speed, brilliant planning and morale. Desperate not to be caught unprepared, as France had been in 1870, all the major powers had detailed, 'hair-trigger' strategic plans to launch sweeping offensive actions against their opponents. The most famous of these was the German Schlieffen Plan to knock out France in six weeks. But the French had their version, Plan 17, to strike at Germany. The Russians had their Plan B, and the Austro-Hungarian forces were similarly prepared. For these plans to succeed against mass armies, the new generation of fortifications, and the power of modern weapons, they required huge offensive forces. The period from 1911 to 1914 saw an increasingly desperate build-up of military strength in terms of men, armaments and strategic railways that virtually guaranteed the final catastrophe.

The expansion of armies to unprecedented levels was made possible by the European population explosion of the nineteenth century and an advanced railway network to transport them. Between 1800 and 1914 the population of most European countries doubled, in Britain and Russia it quadrupled. Between 1912 and 1914 Germany increased its army from 515,000 to 890,000. The French, with a much smaller population, responded in 1913 by an increase in the length of service for their conscripts which raised their army from 545,000 to 735,000. In 1913 the Russian army launched the modernisation and expansion of its army from 1,200,000 to 1,700,000. At the same time French financiers, under the prompting of their government, provided funds for the expansion of 3,000 miles of strategic railway lines from the interior of Russia to the German and Austro-Hungarian borders. Only Austria-Hungary, of the great continental powers, failed to keep pace in this deadly numbers game. Austro-Hungarian forces numbered nearly 400,000 but they were about to be overtaken by their deadly enemy, the newly expanded Serbia. Britain, with a much smaller army, was prepared to commit to the fray an expeditionary force of 100,000, with a further 200,000 within 40 days of the outbreak of war. Yet the paradox of the increasing size of the European armies was that the sheer weight of numbers on both sides, and the inflexible nature of railway transport, would prevent the sweeping movements upon which the plans were based. Mass armies on this scale would cover hundreds of square miles and would overcrowd and block the restricted theatre of operations of north west Europe. For all their meticulous preparation, the grand strategic plans were incapable of delivering the quick, decisive victory for which they had been designed.

8 The Shaping of Public Opinion

> **KEY ISSUE** How did public opinion play an increasingly important role in the conduct of military affairs in the period up to 1914?

As we have seen in earlier sections, public opinion could have a significant effect on the conduct of war. What was a new and dangerous feature in the decades leading up to 1914 was the growing intensity of warlike public opinion in peacetime. By the time of the Crimean War the telegraph had brought even distant conflicts to the daily attention of the reading public. As the century wore on there was an increased readership of newspapers at all levels of society, and an increase in literacy in all European countries. Literacy rates had more than doubled due to deliberate government programmes for free, compulsory education. In fact one of the driving forces for state education was the military motive. In the technological age an educated soldier was a more effective soldier. In the 1870s following the Prussian victories, which many ascribed to a better-educated conscript army, a wave of wide-ranging educational reforms was passed by the major powers of Europe. Therefore as a whole the population of Europe was more educated and more open to new ideas than ever before.

a) Patriotism and Social Darwinism

Europe's traditional leaders had grave reservations about the education of the masses. On the one hand there were obvious military and economic benefits in an educated workforce, but on the other hand the population, or certain elements of it, might be subverted by explosive new ideas. New political ideas like liberalism or socialism could divide populations along class lines, while nationalism and patriotism united the population. This unifying aspect of patriotism was played upon by politicians and newspapermen alike to bind together people whose lives had been buffeted by the changes associated with industrialisation. Patriotism was to be the glue to hold increasingly fluid populations together. The late nineteenth century was the age of nation-building with new flags, anthems and loyalties.

Unfortunately there could be a darker side to patriotism. To believe that one's own country is best can also lead to a belief that other countries and peoples are inferior and can be conquered and exploited. This view was sometimes called Social Darwinism as it attempted to apply Charles Darwin's views on evolution and the 'survival of the fittest' to nations and peoples. It claimed that populations and nations were superior or inferior to each other and that it was natural and right that this would be proven on the battlefield. The individual and the nation would find their glorious destiny in war. Von Moltke, the 'victor of Sedan' and a heroic figure to subsequent generations of Germans, expressed a widely held sentiment when he declared:

> War is an element of the divine order of the world. In it are developed the noblest virtues of man: courage and self-denial, fidelity to duty and the spirit of sacrifice; soldiers give their lives. Without war, the world would stagnate and lose itself in materialism.[7]

b) Militarism

In some countries the population's identification with the military went further than just pride in their activities. After 1871 more men had to do army training either with the regular army or the reserves, and this led to military values, and a respect for the army, being

French cartoon of a child gazing at the 'lost provinces' of Alsace and Lorraine and the historic call for revenge.

drilled into vast numbers across Europe. This process was called militarism. Its roots ran deepest in Germany but it could be seen in most European countries. The army was no longer the dumping ground for misfits and the underclass: mass conscription meant that all classes were represented in it, and all sections of society could take pride in it. This mass identification of the nation with its armed forces was a dangerous new ingredient in public life. In mobilising mass public opinion, politicians had created a Frankenstein's monster that could not always be contained. From Disraeli's government (1874–80) onwards Britons had been taught to revere the Empire and the undisputed power of the Royal Navy upon which it depended. When German naval building challenged that supremacy the rivalry became a burning public issue, forcing the hand of the British government into an ill-tempered contest with Germany, which, more than any other factor, provoked bitter Anglo-German hostility. The cause of the lost provinces of Alsace and Lorraine (taken by Prussia after the Franco-Prussian War) for French public opinion, and the fate of Slav peoples outside Russia (Pan-Slavism) for Russian national identity were similarly explosive issues. In times of crisis governments found that their hands were tied. The involvement of public opinion had raised the stakes, and made international negotiations and crisis management far more difficult. Wars were harder to avoid.

We must be careful not to assume that all Europeans were imbued with an ultra-nationalistic, war-like frenzy. There were pacifist movements across the continent especially in left wing and religious circles. By 1912 the German Socialist Party was the largest party in the country and seen as dangerously anti-militarist (and therefore unpatriotic) by Germany's military and political leaders. But these sentiments could not withstand the unrelenting glorification of war, the honour of serving, and possibly dying, for one's country and the portrayal of the villainy of one's rivals. From 1890 militaristic pressure groups sprang up to demand greater spending on the military and received mass support. The German Naval League attracted over a million members, its British counterpart over 100,000. Militaristic youth movements, and team games in schools, were established to promote physical fitness and the acceptance of military values and discipline. Even the Boy Scouts had military connotations. The full version of its motto 'Be Prepared' is actually:

> 'Be prepared to die for your country ... so that when the time comes you may charge home with confidence, not caring whether you are to be killed or not.'[8]

As the memory of real warfare became more distant, participation in war was seen as honourable, an adventure, even a lark. Such attitudes among Europe's population made it easier for their leaders to take them into the disaster of 1914 and to continue the war for four and a half years despite its massive losses and costs.

9 Conclusion

> **KEY ISSUE** What impact did industrialisation have on the nature of warfare during this period?

The traditional leaders of Europe must have hoped and expected that once they had finally overcome Napoleon they could return to the political and military securities of the eighteenth century. Indeed for 30 years this appeared to be the case, but as the century wore on Europe was to be shaken by forces every bit as disruptive as those ushered in by Napoleon. Industrialisation and nationalism transformed Europe and her military establishments. Industrialisation produced a succession of technological developments in communications and armaments that revolutionised the conduct of war. On a wider level industrialisation produced mass societies that were more organised, productive and wealthy than ever before. In its turn this facilitated a population explosion that allowed the dream, or nightmare, of mass peacetime armies to become a reality. Industrialisation also led to more urbanised, literate societies that were 'informed' on international and military matters by a burgeoning mass media and populist politicians. Just as industrialisation led to the greater organisation of resources, so it enabled a greater control over shared beliefs about society, the nation and war. In the decades leading up to 1914 public opinion became increasingly nationalistic and militaristic and took lightly, or even supported, the idea of a general European war.

References

1   A. Bold, *The Martial Muse* (Pergamon press, 1976), p. 99.
2   T. Standage, *The Victorian Internet* (Phoenix, 1999), p. 146.
3   M. Howard, *The Franco-Prussian War* (Methuen, 1981), p. 2.
4   B. Bond, *The Pursuit of Victory* (Oxford, 1996), p.70.
5   J. Ellis, *The Social History of the Machine Gun* (Pimlico, 1976), p. 94.
6   J.F.C. Fuller, *The Conduct Of War* (Da Capo, 1992), p.156.
7   B. Bond *War and Society in Europe 1870–1970* (Sutton, 1984), p. 26.
8   Bond, *War and Society in Europe,* p. 75.

Summary Diagram
Technological Advance and Tactical Conservatism

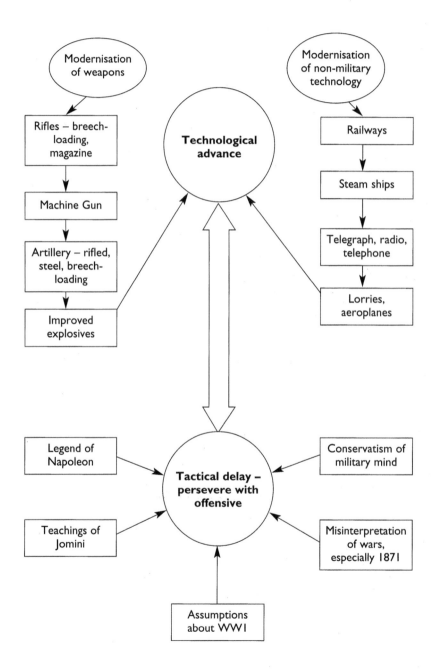

Answering structured and essay questions on Chapter 4

This chapter covers a long period of time and questions will often deal with issues which span the whole period. These issues could include the impact of industrialisation, the growing importance of public opinion, and the technological advances in weaponry and communications and their impact on the nature of warfare. Here are some examples that require you to draw information from across the whole period.

Structured questions are designed to lead you on from the presentation of relevant factual information in the early questions to a wider, more analytical account in the final question. Consider the following:

a) What are the improvements in weapons technology and what impact do they have in the period 1815–1914? *(10 marks)*

b) What other changes took place between 1815 and 1914 to ensure that wars between major powers would be highly destructive of life? *(20 marks)*

For the first of these, you need to provide a brief description of the innovations and improvements to rifles, artillery, the machine gun and explosives which increased their range, accuracy and firepower.

For b), extend your answer to include all other developments which increased the scale and destructiveness of war. This should include: non-military developments such as railways and the telegraph; organisational changes following the example of Prussia; assumptions (often mistaken) made about future wars; attitudes and beliefs among leaders and populations that encouraged war and allowed for mass participation.

Typical essay questions include the following:

1. During the period 1815–1914 why did tactics not keep pace with advances in weapons technology?

This essay deals with the 'cultural lag' between the introduction of new weapons, transport and communication technology and an appropriate tactical response by the military. The information required for this essay is provided in outline form in the Summary Diagram on page 73.

2. What part does public opinion play in the conduct of war from 1792 to 1914?

Note that this question requires knowledge from the previous chapter. Your answer needs to explain the increasing importance of public opinion and governments' attempts to shape it. Provide examples of this as well as reasons for the 'widening' of public opinion due to changes in society brought about by industrialisation. These factors include: increased literacy rates and the expanded readership of newspapers; the growth of democracy; increased urbanisation; and the development and use of advanced communications. This question could also be extended to 1918.

Study the extract from Moltke on page 69, the full Boy Scouts' motto on page 71 and the French cartoon on page 70. Then answer the following questions:

a) What does Moltke mean when he claims that 'War is an element in the divine order of the world' (page 69, line 1)? *(10 marks)*

b) What do you think was the purpose and effect of the Boy Scouts' motto on the boys in the scouts? *(10 marks)*

c) What message is the French cartoon trying to convey, and what consequences might it have? *(10 marks)*

d) Using all of the sources, as well as your own knowledge, explain what they tell us about the militarisation of public opinion. *(20 marks)*

5 The First World War

POINTS TO CONSIDER

The First World War represents a fundamental change in the nature of warfare. Its scale, intensity and modernity mark it down as a new type of conflict. Although many of its features were foreshadowed in the nineteenth century, they reached their full potential in World War One and were used on a scale unimaginable to people in the previous century. As you work through the chapter focus on those areas of significant change as well as those areas of continuity.

KEY DATES

1914	**August**	Outbreak of war. Launching of the plans of attack. Allied blockade begins.
	September	Failure of the plans of attack.
	December	Trench warfare becomes established.
1915	**March**	Opening of the Gallipoli 'sideshow'.
	April	First use of poison gas at second battle of Ypres. Continuation of mass frontal attacks. Italy enters the war.
1916		Battles of attrition – Verdun and the Somme. Brusilov offensive against Austria.
1917	**February**	Resumption of Germany's unrestricted submarine warfare.
	March	Overthrow of the Tsar.
	April	USA enters the war.
	November	Bolshevik revolution in Russia.
1918	**March**	Russia withdraws from war and signs Treaty of Brest-Litovsk. Ludendorff offensive.
	August	Successful allied counter offensive.
	11 November	Armistice.

1 Introduction: A New Form of War

> **KEY ISSUE** What are the novel features of war in World War One?

World War One represents a fundamental change in the nature of warfare. The war was a combination of new features and those elements that had been developed in the nineteenth century but only reached their full potential during 1914–1918. The degree and intensity of innovation in such a short space of time set the greatest possible challenges to military and political leaders and their societies. The novel features of war were:

- It was the first great artillery war. Artillery was responsible for 70 per cent of all casualties.
- It was the first truly modern, industrial war; its weapons and its very outcome were dependent on industrial innovation and mass production. It was the first war to make use of the internal combustion engine and wireless telegraphy on a mass scale.
- It was the first great aviation and submarine war.
- The destructive power of the weaponry used on all sides was unprecedented.
- It was the first chemical war, involving poison gasses and napalm.
- It was the first war to be truly described as a world war.
- It was the first total war. Whole societies and their economies were mobilised.
- Its scale exceeded all previous wars. It was a mass war with mass armies, mass production and mass casualties.
- The intensity of the war was unprecedented. Battles were longer and involved far more men than in the Napoleonic age or the wars of 1866 and 1870.

2 Strategy: The Failure of the Plans

> **KEY ISSUE** How did the failure of the Schlieffen Plan demonstrate the weakness of strategic planning in the early years of the war?

In the years preceding 1914 military strategists could not foresee the fundamental changes the war would bring. They followed the traditional military course of looking into the past to learn the 'lessons' of 1870. Universally they concluded that the war would be short and that the most rapid mobilisation and the heaviest opening attack would secure victory. All the major continental powers had detailed plans for mass attacks based upon these assumptions. However, due to the superiority of the German armed forces, it was to be the success or failure of the German Schlieffen plan that would decide whether the war was truly to be 'over by Christmas'. In fact all the strategic plans failed long before Christmas, but this did not mean the end of the war, which dragged on for another four years.

The failure of the Schlieffen plan at all levels demonstrates the weakness of strategic planning, not only in the opening encounters, but also throughout the majority of the war. The more fixed and detailed the plans of distant generals the more likely they were to diverge from reality on the ground. Schlieffen's plan was devised in 1905 to solve the age-old Prussian/German problem of how to fight a war on two fronts against France and Russia. His solution was to avoid this by concentrating German forces against France, defeat her in six weeks, and then turn round to deal with Russia. The plan was based upon two crucial assumptions that were more relevant to 1870 than to 1914. The first was that the French war effort would be as weak and disorganised as it had been in 1870. The second assumption was that Russia was so disorganised that their vast army would take nearly two months to mobilise and attack. Yet both of these crucial assumptions were wrong. Schlieffen's plan accepted that an attack on France through their shared border around Alsace and Lorraine would be held up by the mass of French troops, huge French fortifications and a lack of room to manoeuvre. His plan was to avoid this well defended zone and put as much of his 1.5 million strong force as he dared into an unstoppable right hook to swing through neutral Luxembourg and Belgium to encircle Paris from the west. The attack would then return eastwards to crush the main French forces on the German border, where they had been pinned down by German defenders. The plan was the most ambitious and intricate of all the plans of 1914. It had been painstakingly calculated, practised and refined for more than a decade yet it failed at all levels and demonstrated the limits of strategic planning, logistics and communications.

There were several key reasons for the failure of the plan. Politically the plan was naïve and had disastrous consequences. An attack through neutral Belgium would almost certainly bring Britain into the war, as she was a long-standing guarantor of Belgian neutrality. In operational terms the 'unstoppable' right wing was weakened before it was launched. Schlieffen's successor as Commander in Chief, Moltke, withdrew forces from the right hook through Belgium to strengthen defensive forces protecting Germany against possible early Russian and French attacks. In tactical terms the men in Schlieffen's right hook were asked to do the impossible. Most of this force was composed of recent conscripts and reserves, and yet they were required to march 450 miles at a rate of over 20 miles a day while dealing with resistance on the way. The plan's shortcomings also reveal the limits of technology and communications at this time. Railways had transformed the movement of men and supplies but they were inflexible and were vulnerable to sabotage. Essential supplies could not keep pace with the advancing armies. Recent developments in wireless communications promised much but were dangerously unreliable in the thick of war. Quite simply, a strategy that involved the rapid deployment of millions of men and horses required reliable transport and communications on a scale not available for another generation.

All other plans failed before the Schlieffen plan. The French plan of attack through Alsace and Lorraine, Plan 17, saw a mass frontal attack by French troops wearing startling red caps and trousers and blue tunics. The smaller German defensive force repelled the attack,

German infantry make their mass advance to the Marne, August 1914, before the deadlock of trench warfare.

inflicting 300,000 casualties in the first weeks of war. The ambitious Schlieffen plan lasted little longer, held up by redirected French and British armies at the Battle of the River Marne on 9 September. By the same time the Russian's attack on Eastern Prussia (Plan B) was smashed by German counter attacks at Tannenberg and the Masurian Lakes. The Austro-Hungarians' plan of attack against the Russians (which the Germans insisted upon) met the same fate as the Russians' disorganised attack against the Germans. Both defeated armies had suffered in excess of 350,000 casualties and prisoners taken in a matter of weeks. By mid-September 1914 all of the ambitious plans of attack, which were the only plans made by the military, had been shattered. Great battles were won and lost but they could not deliver anything like outright victory. Despite dreadful losses every major participant still had vast numbers in the field with arrangements in place to deliver ever greater numbers. Victory would be a long time in coming.

3 Tactics: Trench Warfare   David + Sam

> **KEY ISSUE** Why did trench warfare become the dominant method of war on the Western Front?

Once the German advance had been checked at the Marne there was a further attempt to restart the war of movement by a series of out-flanking manoeuvres to get round the back of one's opponent. This was the 'Race to the Sea' which resulted in a continuous front reaching from the Channel to the Swiss Alps. No flanks were left; the war of sweeping manoeuvres on the Western Front was over. To hold their position, and to remove themselves from direct fire, both sides dug in to form a continuous series of trenches along the whole of the front. Trenches were not unique to the First World War; they had been used for short periods in the American Civil War and many of the wars of the late nineteenth century. But trench warfare was different in the First World War: it was not a temporary arrangement, or limited to certain battles, it was the dominant form of warfare for the entire Western Front, and much of the Eastern Front, for the majority of the war.

Trench warfare was determined by the technology available to the military, the huge numbers facing each other, and the limited room for manoeuvre on the Western Front. The Front extended for some 700 miles but much of this was unsuitable for the movement of mass armies. The dominant weapons of the time, artillery, magazine rifles and the machine gun, had been developed or improved in the latter part of the nineteenth century to provide greater range, accuracy and fire power. Unprotected troops could not expose themselves to this deadly onslaught of fire for long. They had to take cover, and this meant digging into the ground.

The early trenches were natural ditches or hastily constructed shallow holes, as they were expected to be temporary. As it became apparent that they were likely to be more permanent, they evolved into a sophisticated interlocking defensive network, but also one from which attacks could be launched. Ideally the trenches were positioned on the best defensive location, such as on high ground with a clear view of enemy advances. The Germans had the best of these, often giving ground to secure the most favourable locations. The French and British trenches were designed primarily as pro-tected positions from which to launch an attack. The first trench was the firing and command line, which was positioned anything from 50 to 800 yards from the enemy front line. The deadly space between the two sets of trenches was known as 'No Man's Land'. The line was zigzagged to prevent shell blast or rifle fire down the length of the trench. Twenty yards behind this were deeper 'dug-outs' for basic sleeping accommodation. The second line, some 100 yards back, was the support trench. The third line, 500 yards further back, was the reserve trench with troops held back as reinforcements for defence or attack. The German lines were designed primarily for defence, to allow them to deploy an effective 'elastic defence' with lightly held front lines but a much stronger force held back in the reserve trench.

Trench warfare maximised the power of the defensive. In between the front lines, mines and thick rolls of razor sharp barbed wire 30 yards deep also held up the offensive, although this did not prevent further bloody attacks. Twice as many casualties were inflicted on the attackers as on the defenders. The Western Front had degenerated into a bloody stalemate. 'From the end of 1914 to the spring of 1918 there was no change of more than ten miles in the front lines'.[1] On the Eastern Front, after the dramatic sweeping movements of the opening battles, trench warfare also became established. However, the sheer range of the Eastern Front (more than twice the length of the Western Front but manned by only the same number of men) meant that the positions held were more fluid.

4 Weapons and the Evolution of Tactics

> **KEY ISSUE** How did weapons development in a) Chemicals, b) Tanks, c) Artillery, d) Infantry, e) the Air War lead to a change in tactics?

By 1915, after the breakdown of the plans of movement, the war on the Western Front subsided into the stalemate of trench warfare. Frustrated by this and horrified by the losses, political leaders and military strategists began a search to break the deadlock. If the exist-ing weapons had produced the stalemate on the battlefield then the development of new weapons and tactics might yet achieve break-through.

a) Chemical Warfare *Archie*

One possible solution to the stalemate of the trenches was the use of poison gas. Britain, France and Germany had all considered this in 1914 but it was Germany, with a superior chemical industry, that first used it at Ypres in April 1915. The chlorine gas, carried on the wind toward the British trenches, disabled four miles of the British line. Gas attacks appeared to hold great promise. For the Germans, fighting a war on two fronts, it was seen as a substitute for manpower. Gas had a psychological, as well as physical impact. It retained the element of surprise, it spread panic and it did not destroy the land over which the infantry would advance. 1917 saw the introduction of the more effective phosgene and mustard gasses and shells to deliver the gas on to deeper enemy positions. These proved useful in allied advances in 1918 but even here they were little more than a minor addition to the major weapons of the war. The great disadvantage of a gas attack was that it was dependent on the wind direction and could be blown back in the faces of those who released it. This was the fate of the British at the Battle of Loos in September 1915. In addition to this, all armies rapidly developed and issued protective respirators to their troops. Napalm, in the form of petroleum-based flame throwers, was also developed as a trench-clearing weapon.

b) Tanks *Not transp*

The development of the tank by both the British and the French also led to over-optimistic expectations. The tank seemed to hold out the hope of breaking the deadlock of the trenches by integrating fire-power and mobility with protection against the machine gun. The tank had been made possible by the internal combustion engine and inspired by the caterpillar-tracked tractor. Technologically the tank could not live up to the high expectations placed upon it. The early tanks were slow, vulnerable and unreliable. They had a top speed of five miles an hour on roads but this was reduced to one to two miles an hour over the battleground. Their armour plating was vulnerable to artillery and the Germans also developed an armour-piercing bullet. The tanks made their first appearance at the Battle of the Somme, 1916, where the British used 49 tanks. As there were too few of them, they were widely dispersed and were not co-ordinated effectively with the infantry. Tanks were next used in large numbers (378) with infantry support of 80,000 men at the battle of Cambrai in November 1917. No long preliminary barrage was required as the tanks themselves could flatten or cut through the wire and the tanks needed firm ground. The attack therefore achieved surprise and many German troops fled in terror. However, the attack could not be sustained; many tanks were destroyed and an even greater number broke down. By the end of the battle the British had lost 300 of their 374 tanks and the Germans had retaken most of the ground earlier lost. At Amiens on 8 August 1918 over 400 British tanks were used and helped achieve a significant breakthrough, but four days later only six were still in operation. The French developed their own light tanks, and had over 3,000 by the end of the war, the British having nearly the same number. The Germans were less convinced of their usefulness and produced only 20. The tank's greatest asset was psychological, as when first encountered they led to panic. A German war correspondent reported:

> 1 When the German troops crept out of their dug-outs in the morning and stretched their necks to look for the English, their blood chilled. Mysterious monsters were crawling towards them over the craters ... Nothing stopped them ... someone in the trenches said, 'The devil is
> 5 coming' and word was passed along the line. Tongues of flame leapt from the sides of the iron caterpillars ... the English infantry came in waves behind.'[2]

Local breakthroughs were achieved but quickly reversed as the tanks had a survival rate of just a few days in battle. The tanks revealed great potential, but it was to be the next generation that was to see that potential realised.

c) Artillery

One of the most enduring images of the First World War is the dominance of the machine gun: 'the master of the battlefield' as J.R. Roberts called it.[3] Yet that description is more accurately applied to the artillery. The static nature of much of the war meant that the guns could take up near permanent positions in the most favourable locations. In more mobile wars they had struggled to keep up with the battlefront. Their devastating impact is revealed in the breakdown of casualties. In the Russo-Japanese War artillery fire caused 10 per cent of casualties; in World War One it inflicted 70 per cent. Troops at the front were continuously exposed to artillery fire. As J. Terraine puts it, 'Artillery was the killer; artillery was the terrifier. Artillery followed the soldier to the rear, sought him out in his billet, found him on the march.'[4] The major reason for the huge death toll caused by artillery was the massive number of high explosive shells fired. Literally millions were fired in the days preceding an attack, but bombardment was virtually continuous throughout the war. It has been calculated that even though artillery was the great destroyer it required 1,400 shells fired to achieve each fatality. However, before artillery could reap this grim harvest it had to make fundamental readjustments to the new realities of trench warfare.

At the beginning of the war both sides had the type of artillery required for the predicted war of movement: the quick-firing field gun to support the infantry with shrapnel fire in open battle. Once trench warfare became established they were less useful. They had a flat trajectory of fire and were unlikely to penetrate the trenches. The artillery desperately needed to increase its numbers of howitzers and mortars with their higher, looping angle of fire and the powerful heavy guns with high explosive shells to destroy barbed wire and enemy trenches.

In addition to the wrong type of guns, the artillery also used the wrong tactics. A predictable barrage for a set time was clearly seen as the preliminary to an infantry offensive. The ending of the barrage was an effective call to the defending side to take up firing positions for the inevitable attack. At the same time the bombardment would usually turn the ground to be advanced over into a quagmire. Well defended trenches were not impregnable: they could be taken but there needed to be an overhaul of tactics. Crucially the artillery needed to be integrated into the infantry's attack.

Artillery tactics evolved to become more flexible and scientific and to recapture the element of surprise. Opening barrages were made less predictable and cut short so that the ground would not be rendered impassable and advancing infantry raids could take the enemy unawares. Tunnels were secretly constructed to place massive mines under enemy trenches that were considered impregnable by frontal attack, such as at Messines Ridge in 1917. The creeping barrage was developed and proved one of the most significant developments of the war. This was a barrage that was carefully targeted to slowly move ahead of the advancing infantry, not necessarily to destroy the enemy lines and artillery but to neutralise them, i.e. force them to take cover. A more scientific and accurate approach to the crucial task of destroying enemy artillery and machine gun posts (counter battery fire) was developed. This was particularly noticeable in the increasingly effective British artillery. By these methods the artillery had managed to shift the balance of force on the battlefield from manpower to firepower.

d) The Infantry

i) Attrition

The greatest change in tactics was required of the infantry and their commanders. As we have seen, all armies began the war convinced that massed attack was the only route to success. Emphasis was placed on moral force and spirit over modern weapons. Even after the destruction of these opening offensives and the massive casualties inflicted most commanders clung to the notion of frontal attack. These attacks foundered on the defensive power of the trenches and men died in their hundreds of thousands. Tactics took a darker turn in 1916 when commanders used the certainty of mass casualties in their calculations. The battles at Verdun and the Somme were designed not to achieve significant territorial breakthroughs but simply to tie down and kill as many of the enemy as possible. This was the war of attrition. It intended to break the morale of the enemy and to grind down their numbers. The battles led to mass casualties, but they were roughly equal on both sides, with over 700,000 casualties recorded by both sides at each battle. Years later Corporal W. Shaw gave his recollections of the fighting at the Somme:

> 1 Our artillery had been bombing their line for six days and nights, trying to smash the German barbed-wire entanglements. The result was we never got anywhere near the Germans. Our lads was mown down. They were just simply slaughtered. It was just one continuous go for-
> 5 ward, come back, go forward, come back, losing men all the time and there we were, wondering when it was all going to end. You couldn't do anything. You were either tied down by the shelling or the machine guns and yet we kept at it, kept on going all along the line, making no impact on the Germans at all. We didn't get anywhere, we never moved
> 10 from the line, hardly. The machine guns were levelled and they were mowing the top of the trenches. You daren't put your finger up. The men were just falling back in the trenches. ... It was hopeless. And those young officers, going ahead, they were picked off like flies. We tried to go over and it was just impossible. We were mown down. [5]

ii) The Reintroduction of Mobile Tactics

As the slaughter mounted for little apparent gain, commanders, under political pressure, began to evolve their tactics. The Germans were the first to adapt to the restrictions of trench warfare. During the Battle of the Somme they developed a fluid defensive-offensive that was based upon a lightly held front line prepared to give ground but then to launch an immediate heavy counterattack. Specially selected storm-troops led these counterattacks. By 1917 they were grouped in units of eleven men and were heavily armed with newly developed portable weapons in the form of light machine guns and mortars, grenades and flame-throwers. These well armed rapid strike forces reintegrated firepower and mobility. They would independently sweep through enemy lines leaving strong defensive positions, such as machine gun posts, to be 'mopped up' by the second wave of attackers. The Ludendorff Offensive of March 1918 was the most successful implementation of the German 'infiltration tactics' using manpower released from the Eastern Front after the collapse of Russia. The offensive restored movement to the battlefield. The attack troops had been intensively trained in the new techniques in the months leading up to the attack. Unlike so many previous offensives it was brilliantly co-ordinated with a surprise hurricane artillery bombardment, including gas and smoke shells, and attack aircraft suppressing enemy defences and machine guns. The battlefields of 1918 looked more like those of 1940 than of 1916.

The French and British forces also developed mobile infiltration tactics. The Germans picked out and trained only a minority of troops as storm-troopers but it meant that the German second wave of attack was of a lower quality and petered out after big early advances. In contrast the British trained all of their troops in the new techniques. By 1918 the British troops had moved away from the long linear advance; their attacking force was now built around a heavily armed, mobile, semi-independent platoon of 40 men. These units advanced in rushes, taking advantage of cover and shell holes and adopted a diamond formation covering as much as 100 yards to reduce the danger of shells. The troops were trained and specialised in their particular task and armed with weapons developed during the war. The men in the platoon were divided into machine gunners, equipped with the new, lighter Lewis machine gun; bombers, equipped with hand grenades; rifle bombers, using the new grenade firers; and riflemen. Flame-throwers were used for trench clearing operations. With the great array of destructive new weapons, it is tempting to see the First World War as a depersonalised war of long-range modern weaponry and the men as mere operators of this new technology. We must remember, however, that this war, like all wars, was a bewildering mixture of new and old. When troops stormed enemy trenches on night raids, the most effective weapons were not necessarily the modern ones, nor even the rifle with fixed bayonet, which was too unwieldy in the cramped conditions of the trench. Instead troops improvised their own 'medieval' weapons for hand-to-hand fighting, such as heavy clubs or sharpened short trench spades to be used as battle axes.

The allied counter attacks of July and August 1918 had the advantage of surprise, sophisticated artillery cover, hundreds of tanks and over 1,000 aeroplanes, including bombers, ground attack planes, supply and reconnaissance craft. To keep the momentum going, armoured cars, faster light tanks, motorcycle machine guns and troop-carrying lorries drove deep into enemy positions. At last the attacks were co-ordinated, flexible and mobile. They broke through the German lines and shattered the deep-lying Hindenburg Line. The battle tactics of the Second World War had emerged at the very end of the First World War.

e) The War in the Air

The air war represents the most outstanding example of the rapid development of a new technology under the intense pressure of war. All the major powers entered the war with only basic air services amounting to a combined total of only 200–300 aircraft, which were slow reconnaissance planes. By 1918 that number had risen to over

A mass 'dog-fight' over the Western Front. The slow speed of the planes allowed for close manoeuvrability unmatched in any subsequent conflict.

8,000 with a personnel of 300,000 and supplied by hundreds of thousands of workers to manufacture the planes. The aircraft had become an integral feature of total war.

In the opening period of mobile war, reconnaissance aeroplanes provided useful information on the movement of armies. As the war evolved into trench warfare they were the only means of gaining information on the position of enemy artillery and reserves, displacing the historic function of the cavalry. Fighter aircraft evolved as a means of denying the enemy this invaluable information. As pilots took on the role of bombing and the pursuit of enemy craft so planes became more specialised: heavier and sturdier for bombing, and lighter for pursuit and combat. At the beginning of the war the pilots were armed only with pistols and hand grenades. The major breakthrough of 1915 was the development of a fixed, forward-firing machine gun which was synchronised to fire through the spaces between the revolving propeller blades. This turned the aircraft into a flying gun.

The relatively short period of the air war with its individual 'dogfights' in tiny, highly manoeuvrable planes gave rise to the legend of the air aces. The legend persisted even though the individual air ace was to be overwhelmed by mass warfare in the same way his ground-based counterpart had been. The increased production of planes led to the evolution of massed fighter tactics in which romantic individual action gave way to concentrated attack formations, such as the German 'flying circuses' of as many as 60 aeroplanes. All of the original air aces died in the new phase of mass air actions. In 1917 in what became known as 'Bloody April' the British Royal Flying Corps suffered losses of 30 per cent a week! The air war, just like the ground war, was to be decided by resources and mass production and it was the allies who were able to produce more replacement planes and flyers than the Germans.

The original function of the fighter plane was to achieve dominance of the skies for its reconnaissance planes, but increasingly the fighter was used for ground attack purposes. The fighters were used to attack trenches, suppress infantry advances and disable enemy supplies and gun positions. The Germans developed an armoured plane for this purpose, but losses to all sides were huge with more than 50 per cent losses in pilots. By 1918 aircraft proved a useful, but not decisive, element in the allied breakthrough. Strategic bombing of targets on the home front of the enemy had begun with the Zeppelin raids against Britain in May 1915. Heavier bomber planes replaced these vulnerable craft in 1917. The British responded with the development of their own bomber fleet as part of the newly established independent Royal Air Force. Britain, France and Italy made bombing raids into enemy territory in 1918 but the results were limited. Nevertheless the fateful conviction that bombing civilians could undermine the enemy's morale and potentially end wars was one of the lessons taken from the First World War to be ruthlessly applied in the Second World War. Modern technology had extended the killing zone to the home front.

5 Leadership: 'The Donkeys'?

> **KEY ISSUE** Do the commanders of the First World War deserve their reputation as 'butchers and bunglers'?

The most contentious issue arising from the First World War is that of leadership. The stalemate on the Western Front, the repeated disastrous attacks and the unprecedented losses have led to an intense scrutiny of the role of the Generals.

a) Germany

The German leadership is often hailed as the best in the war. Yet we have already seen how its only plan (Schlieffen), despite ten years of detailed preparation, failed at every level. Also the German forces were as likely to send mass attacks against heavily armed defenders as any other army was. For the first half of the war the German army did have an advantage in leadership and trained manpower because it possessed a large standing professional army that was well equipped and fought the war according to the German army's plan of attack. A major strength of the German leadership was its ability to delegate command downwards and harness flexibility and individual fighting skills. Again this was made possible by the highly trained German army at lower levels. However, this advantage only lasted as long as the original German army lasted. After 1916, and the massive losses at Verdun and the Somme, that army had been wiped out and the German army was now reduced to a new civilian army, just as Britain's had been since late in 1914. It no longer had the edge. Ludendorff was considered the best general of the war for his sweeping victories on the Eastern Front at Tannenberg and the Masurian Lakes. He almost pulled off an even more remarkable last-ditch victory with the 'Ludendorff offensive' in March 1918. But later that year, Ludendorff, like Moltke before him four years previously, had a breakdown and loss of will that hastened the German defeat.

b) France and Britain

The French commanders are most identified with suicidal mass frontal attacks. In the first weeks of war Joffre lost 300,000 troops in what appeared to be futile Napoleonic attacks. In Nivelle's 1917 offensive France lost 120,000 in the opening two days which sparked a mutiny that involved half of the French army. But in British military history it is the role of the British commanders, especially General Haig, that still arouses passionate controversy. British commanders were attacked for their inflexibility and failure to adapt to the changed circumstances of trench warfare. This also led to a charge of failing to adopt the newer weapons of war, such as the machine gun and the tank, and sticking with the costly infantry tactics of attack over a broad front. To their critics the massive casualty rate in the battles of attrition for little ground gained is evidence of a callous disregard for human suffering. The criticism of the British commanders, and Haig in particular, began even before the war ended. Lloyd George was their most high profile critic, but the impression was reinforced by the anti-war poets and writers, and post war strategists, such as J.F.C. Fuller and Liddell Hart. Siegfried Sassoon's poem 'The General' created a lasting impression:

1   'Good-morning; good-morning!' the General said
    When we met him last week on our way to the line.
    Now the soldiers he smiled at are most of 'em dead,
    And we're cursing his staff for incompetent swine.
5   'He's a cheery old card', grunted Harry to Jack
    As they slogged up to Arras with rifle and pack.
       . . . . .
    But he did for them both by his plan of attack.[6]

The criticism reached new levels of vitriol in the 1960s with Alan Clark's 1961 book *The Donkeys*, which took its title from a supposed conversation between Generals Ludendorff and Hoffman.

> Ludendorff: 'The English soldiers fight like lions.'
> Hoffman: 'True. But don't we know that they are lions led by donkeys.'[7]

The 1960s also saw the highly influential theatre and film version of 'Oh What a Lovely War' which ridiculed the bumbling incompetence of the British generals when set against the suffering of their men. This was followed in 1988 by John Laffin's book whose argument is summed up in its title – *British Butchers and Bunglers of World War One*. The image of the bungling British leadership had become so culturally accepted that even the television comedy *Blackadder Goes Forth* could successfully be staged against the ludicrous incompetence of the 'Chateau Generals.' After all, as Captain Blackadder said, the whole purpose of the war was to move General Haig's drinks cabinet ten yards nearer to Berlin.

Although this image remains firmly rooted in the national consciousness, many modern writers, including John Terraine, Paddy Griffith and Peter Simkins, vehemently reject the blanket 'myth' of British command incompetence. These are the new revisionists who seek to 'debunk the debunkers,' namely Clark and Laffin. The revisionists claim that the blanket condemnation of the British Generals denies the fact that the British army under the guidance of its commanders made tremendous improvements, which they could only achieve after hard, bitter experience. The British army at the beginning of the war was a small colonial army that had to take on the strongest army in the world, which was more than 30 times its size. Yet the British army and its leadership grew in strength and sheer fighting ability to take over from the French after Verdun as Germany's deadliest enemy. The Allied leadership knew that they could not remain on the defensive, it was politically unacceptable and it would allow the German army to transfer troops to the Eastern Front to knock Russia out of the war. The German army had to be held in the West and worn down by Allied offensives. Without wonder-weapons to achieve a mobile victory the Allied leadership could only resort to battles of attrition. These battles produced staggering losses on both sides but they inflicted such damage on the German forces that they prepared the way for victory in 1918. In the final defeat of the German army it was the British and Empire forces that achieved the most telling victories with their improved tactics, their readiness to take up new technology, and their delegated command.

6 Morale and the Propaganda War

> **KEY ISSUES** What was the difference between propaganda from above and propaganda from below? What impact did propaganda have on the outcome of the war?

As we have seen in the previous chapter, the years leading up to 1914 were marked by an outpouring of increasingly aggressive nationalistic propaganda. This had helped to reinforce military values in society and psychologically prepare the civilian population for war. Once the war had begun motivation and exaggerated passions were not difficult to arouse. Early propaganda portrayed the honour of one's cause and the barbarity of the enemy. God was enlisted by every army; the massive German force that smashed into neutral Belgium had the words 'Gott mit uns' (God with us) forged on to their belt buckles. After the failure of the opening plans of attack and the deadlock of trench warfare, nations and their leaders realised they were in for the long haul. The war was not going to be decided quickly by professional armies; many of those armies had been wiped out. Even greater armies had to be raised and supplied by civilians, both men and women. Mass warfare called for a mass, willing contribution from combatant societies. Propaganda was now essential to bind societies together for unquestioning sacrifice and effort. Just as total war was to require the mobilisation of men, labour and supplies, so it also demanded the mobilisation of minds.

a) Propaganda from Below

In increasingly urbanised, literate societies, with advanced means of

RED CROSS OR IRON CROSS?

WOUNDED AND A **PRISONER**
OUR SOLDIER CRIES FOR WATER.

THE GERMAN "SISTER"
POURS IT ON THE GROUND BEFORE HIS EYES.

THERE IS NO WOMAN IN BRITAIN
WHO WOULD DO IT.

THERE IS NO WOMAN IN BRITAIN
WHO WILL FORGET IT.

British poster portrays German cruelty as the Kaiser and his General smile on approvingly. This poster was deliberately targeted at inspiring hatred and determination in British women.

communication and entertainment, propaganda entered every home. The greater volume of propaganda, and certainly the most effective, originated not from official government sources but from independent agencies, commercial interests, community groups and individuals. This was presented via newspapers, posters, cartoons, postcards, and souvenirs such as Kitchener beer mugs, ceramic tanks and toys for children. Influential community figures such as teachers, youth leaders and clergymen added their voice. Commercial interests realised that adverts, which associated their product with the war effort, certainly did not harm their sales figures. The major forms of entertainment, the cinema, the music hall, and the gramophone and sheet music industry, played an important role in keeping up morale by playing on the usual motivations of the justice and honour of one's cause and the villainy of the enemy. Both sides commonly used the exaggerated (or invented) atrocity story. The incessant message from all sections of society represented the greatest advertising campaign in history up to that date. The effect of this barrage of propaganda was to intensify the public's identification with the war effort. As a result of this, it was virtually impossible for governments to attempt a negotiated peace settlement for anything less than total victory. It would be a fight to the finish.

b) Propaganda from Above

In 1917 the American senator Hiram Johnson famously claimed that 'The first casualty when war comes, is truth'.[8] Certainly there was official censorship of 'sensitive' information; but propaganda to be effective could not be a byword for lies, it had to be based on a generally accepted truth. That 'truth' might then be shaped, exaggerated and invested with intense emotion, but essentially it had to connect with its audience. The success of propaganda from non-government sources was that it directly tapped in to the intense hopes, prejudices and fears of populations drawn into total war. The more successful government propaganda followed the lead provided by influential campaigns and opinion formed from below. Governments adopted these messages or supported their transmission. The British government did not even see the need for a government propaganda organisation for the home front until 1918. In contrast German propaganda came from above, was more heavy-handed and subsequently less effective. By 1917 the military leaders of Germany recognised the importance of the cinema to morale on the home front and banned American newsreels about the war, replacing them with more 'reliable' German productions. To keep cinemas open during the fuel shortages of 1917–18 they were given priority for coal and electricity supplies. At the Front the major combatants had hundreds of 'field' cinemas for entertainment and morale. However, morale was far more affected by basic material issues, such as the regular rotation of troops in the front line to provide much needed relief, and the provision of adequate food and alcohol supplies.

c) The Impact of Propaganda

The impact of propaganda on the outcome of the war is a contentious issue. Undoubtedly, successful propaganda reinforced unity and determination, its weight and intensity suppressing pacifist or opposition voices. General Ludendorff claimed that the twin reasons for the German defeat in 1918 were the impact of the British blockade and allied propaganda leading to severe hardship and self-doubt. Others have argued that this claim in itself is propaganda intended to divert attention away from the real reason for the German collapse, namely its comprehensive defeat on the battlefield. Another claim for the impact of government-directed propaganda was the British and French conversion of the Americans to enter the war on the allied side. Sophisticated as this approach was, it paled into insignificance beside the impact of Germany's mistreatment of Belgian civilians and its resort to unrestricted submarine warfare that resulted in the loss of American lives.

Another aspect of propaganda by government agencies was the encouragement and funding of separatist or opposition movements inside the enemy camp. This was not a new strategy; it had been attempted in the Revolutionary and Napoleonic period. In the First World War it achieved far greater results. Western propaganda targeted nationalist groups inside the rapidly disintegrating Austro-Hungarian Empire. The Central Powers played the same card by trying to exploit nationalist ambitions within the British and French Empires, especially in Ireland and India. But it was in Russia that Germany achieved its most spectacular, if rather unexpected, success. From March 1915 Germany had been supplying considerable funds to separatist and revolutionary groups in Russia with the intention of sowing discord and division in the Russian war effort. In April 1917, after the fall of the Russian Tsar, the German authorities seized the opportunity of transporting exiled Russian revolutionary leaders, including Lenin, across German held territory and back into Russia. The political, economic and military disintegration of Russia, helped in part by Lenin's propaganda effort, led to the collapse of Russia's Provisional Government and the take-over of the Bolsheviks. Lenin was immediately prepared to make peace with Germany at any price and German policy appeared to have achieved the greatest propaganda coup of the war. The significance of this event and the importance attached to the impact of propaganda by analysts after the war meant that the propaganda effort was to become a major preoccupation in all future wars.

The German Foreign Minister, von Kühlmann, sent the following telegram to army headquarters 3 December 1917.

1 The disruption of the Entente and the subsequent creation of political combinations agreeable to us constitute the most important war aim of our diplomacy. Russia appeared to be the weakest link in the chain, the task therefore was gradually to loosen it, and when possible, to remove
5 it. This was the purpose of the subversive activity we caused to be carried out in Russia behind the front – in the first place promotion of separatist tendencies and support of the Bolsheviks. It was not until the Bolsheviks had received from us a steady flow of funds through various channels and under different labels that they were in a position to be able
10 to build up their main organ, *Pravda*, to conduct energetic propaganda

and appreciably to extend the originally narrow basis of their party. The Bolsheviks have now come to power; how long they will retain power cannot yet be foreseen. They need peace in order to strengthen their own position; on the other hand, it is entirely in our interest that we should exploit the period while they are in power, which may be a short one, to attain firstly an armistice and then, if possible, peace.[9]

15

Punch cartoon, December 1917: the Bolshevik lures 'Russia' into the arms of Germany.

7 Resources and Economic Warfare

> **KEY ISSUE** What are the two levels on which economic warfare was conducted?

Economic warfare, like the propaganda war, was not new. It had played an important part in the Napoleonic Wars. It was to play an even more crucial role in determining the outcome of the First World War. In the first truly industrialised war the industrial mass production of arms and ammunition would prove decisive and would require the total mobilisation of the entire nation and its resources.

The struggle of economies was conducted on two levels;

a) The most effective organisation of one's economy, workforce and resources to supply the war effort.
b) The disruption of the enemy economy; to block supplies reaching the enemy's war effort, including food supplies to the enemy army and workforce.

a) Economic Co-ordination for Total War

As the vast material demands of war in the industrial age became apparent all major combatants began the transformation of their societies from civilian to war economies. In August 1914 the British government introduced the Defence of the Realm Act (DORA) which extended government power over the economy, as well as in other areas of society. This was achieved in a spirit of co-operation with the trade unions and avoided the wholesale drafts of civilian labour. DORA was extended several times to cover price controls, the allocation of labour, railways, the mines, shipping, subsidies for agriculture, and in 1918 food rationing. Britain was not alone in introducing these measures, known universally as war socialism. All combatant countries increasingly turned to women workers to replace enlisted men and to produce munitions. Crucially both Britain and France had the strategic and economic advantage of access to a world-wide empire. Consequently neither suffered the extreme shortages that Germany, Austria-Hungary and Russia had to endure. For Russia three years of total war were to prove too great a strain for the Russian economy to bear. Inflation ran out of control, food supplies to the towns and cities dried up and by late 1916 the Russian railway system had virtually collapsed. By 1917 Russia faced economic and political meltdown; revolution and withdrawal from the war followed rapidly in its wake. Imperial Russia had clearly failed what Arthur Marwick has termed 'the Test of War'.[10]

The Central Powers did not have the material, or manpower, support of an extensive overseas empire. Lack of resources proved to be the Achilles' heel for the German war effort. As the Reich imported nearly half of its foodstuffs and raw materials it was inevitable that a long protracted war and the effects of the British blockade would prove disastrous for Germany. Throughout the war Germany struggled to overcome this fundamental weakness. During this time the military took an increasingly powerful role in government under the guise of organising the war effort. In August 1914 the War Raw Materials Office (KRA) was set up for the purchase and distribution of raw materials, and controls were extended over the labour force. By January 1915 ration cards for food and price controls were established. Between 1916 and 1918 the army, under the direction of Hindenburg and Ludendorff, increased its control over the economy, national policy and the war effort to such an extent that Martin Kitchen has described this episode as the 'silent dictatorship'.[11]

b) Economic Blockade

Britain's great historic strength was based upon its naval supremacy, which, as demonstrated in the Napoleonic wars, could ensure the supply of food and war materials to herself and her coalition partners and deny them to her enemies. If the war continued for longer than the nine months which German strategists had envisaged, then this factor would assume vital significance in determining the outcome of the war. From the outbreak of hostilities Britain adopted a distant blockade from the security of its naval bases in the Channel and at Scapa Flow, to the north of Scotland. All German ships were considered legitimate targets and neutral ships were prevented from supplying any materials to Germany and her allies that Britain defined as contraband. In February 1916 the Ministry of Blockade was established to tighten the noose around the neck of the Central powers. It soon extended the definition of contraband from weapons to include metals, oils, cotton, wool and foods. As with bombing raids, the legitimate targets of total war were being redefined to include the civilian. The rationale was simple and deadly: if whole societies were involved in the war effort, then all parts of that society, military, economic and civilian, could be attacked, disrupted and starved. The number of German civilian deaths caused by the blockade has been put as high as 750,000.[12] Supplies to the military were preserved as much as they could be, but by 1918 food shortages were affecting the operational effectiveness of the Central Powers. Perhaps the most significant aspect of the blockade on the Central Powers was its political and psychological impact. The united front at home was undermined by starvation. Hunger and shortages led to calls for peace and provoked political and social division in Germany and terminal national divisions in Austria-Hungary. From 1916 onwards there were hundreds of food riots and strikes culminating in the great strike of January 1918 in which half a million German workers participated.

c) The German Response

The German response to the British blockade was to attempt one of their own. The German surface fleet could not match the Royal Navy, so in February 1915 Germany made the fateful decision to use submarines to blockade the waters around Britain and Ireland. As Tirpitz said, 'England wants us to starve, we can play the same game'. This led to the sinking of the British liner *Lusitania* in May 1915 with the loss over 1,000 lives, including 128 Americans, and helped push neutral United States towards Britain. On 31 January 1917 the Germans decided on a desperate gamble, a kind of Schlieffen plan of the sea – to impose unrestricted submarine warfare on all supplies bound for Britain and thereby to starve Britain out of the war before American supplies could prove decisive. The tactic produced critical losses of food and supplies to Britain but it also meant the sinking of American ships. The gamble failed, Britain and the U.S. were able to develop effective defensive counter-measures and Britain was not forced out of the war. The German action had ensured not only the economic contribution of America but also its direct military involvement on the allied side in April 1917. The massive morale boost of the entry of the Americans, with their potential for almost limitless supplies, funds and fresh troops, was likely to be decisive in itself. The Central powers could no longer evade the inevitable logic of the imbalance of resources. The German economy, weakened by the blockade, could no longer meet the demands of total war for herself and her industrially underdeveloped allies. The Central powers produced 19 per cent of the world's manufacturing output, the allies over 65 per cent. The allies' population figures dwarfed those of the Central powers and their allies. Tim Travers sums this up, 'Whether in artillery, ammunition supplies, tanks, planes, Lewis guns, rifle grenades, machine guns, food supplies, rail lines, or even horses, the allies were irresistibly superior'.[13] As Ludendorff said despairingly in September 1918, 'We cannot fight against the whole world'.

8 Casualties

> **KEY ISSUES** What countries suffered the greatest casualties in the conflict? What were the long term consequences of these losses?

Casualty figures for the First World War cannot be exact. Casualties include all those who were withdrawn from the battle zone whether through death, sickness or injury. In the case of injuries these could range from life-long disability to wounds of varying severity, often allowing men to rejoin the war where they might become one of the casualty figures once again. Deaths accounted for one-third to one-quarter of all casualties. It has been estimated by various sources that the total number of deaths lies somewhere between 10 and 13 million. Germany and Russia each lost 2 million dead. Germany also lost a further 750,000 civilian deaths as a result of the blockade. Austria-Hungary suffered 1.2 million deaths, the USA 115,000 and Italy 580,000. Britain lost 725,000 dead and a further 250,000 from the empire and France lost 1,322,000.

Beyond these bare statistics lies a human tragedy of almost unimaginable proportions. The psychological and political impact of these losses shaped the rest of the twentieth century. For France victory seemed indistinguishable from defeat; during the war France mobilised 8.4 million men of whom nearly 60 per cent were either killed or wounded. France's population declined during the inter-war period due to the loss of a generation of potential fathers. Psychologically France knew they could not pay such a cost again. For Italy the losses suffered with such little reward in territory at the ensuing peace conference became known as the 'mutilated victory' and was a major factor in the overthrow of the parliamentary system by Mussolini's Fascists. Hitler's Nazi party was able to feed off similar resentments in Germany. In the USA the unacceptable losses, in what many saw as a European civil war, led to a return to isolationism and non-participation in the League of Nations. For Russia, Austria-Hungary and Turkey, defeat and the losses incurred led to the disintegration of their centuries-old empires and the creation of new nations in their wake. From the wreckage of Imperial Russia arose the first communist state. In Britain the casualties were referred to as the 'lost generation' and the revulsion and despair at such sacrifice inspired a widespread pacifist movement which played a significant part in Britain's foreign policy and rearmament of the 1930s.

9 Conclusion

> **KEY ISSUE** What were the areas of change and continuity in the nature of warfare represented by the First World War?

In many ways the First World War represents a fundamental shift in the nature of warfare yet, as with all conflicts, there was an intriguing balance between new and old elements of war. There were many novel features of war such as the air war, the submarine war and new weapons notably the tank and gas. Yet there were also many features that World War One shares with previous conflicts. Although new weapons were developed for the war they were generally ineffective and played a secondary role to those weapons developed and improved in the nineteenth century. The dominant weapons of the war remained the artillery, the rifle and the machine gun. The propaganda war and the war of economies reached new heights but in both there were clear echoes of Britain's struggle with Napoleon a century before. The strategy of the war was similarly backward looking as all sides tried to apply the lessons of the Prussian style of war from the 1860s. When this failed whole armies were forced into trench warfare and a bloody war of attrition which would have been familiar to troops in previous ages.

The greatest changes in the nature of warfare were those brought about by the unprecedented scale and intensity of the war. The war with over 80 per cent of the world's population formally at war is the first that can genuinely be described as a world war. The full mobilisation of advanced industrial techniques and mass production represents the first modern industrial war and produced a quantity of weapons unimaginable to previous generations. Battles could now rage with ferocious intensity for months at a time without exhausting supplies. The demands on production and manpower required a total war effort that brought the civilian into the heart of the conflict. The greater scale and intensity of the war, and the wider involvement of the civilian, produced the most memorable novel feature of the war, the unprecedented level of casualties.

References

1 S.C. Tucker, *The Great War* (UCL Press, 1998), p. 37.
2 A. Lloyd, *The War in the Trenches* (Wordsworth, 2002).
3 J.R. Roberts, *Europe 1880–1945* (Longman, 1990), p. 281.
4 J. Terraine, *The Smoke and the Fire: Myths and Anti-myths of War* (Leo Cooper, 1992), p. 132.
5 L. Macdonald, *1914–1918: Voices and Images of the Great War* (Penguin, 1991), pp. 155–6.
6 A. Bold, *The Martial Muse* (Pergamon Press, 1976), p. 120.
7 A. Clark, *The Donkeys* (Pimlico, 1961), Front papers.
8 P. Knightly, *The First Casualty* (Piron, 2000), p. xi.
9 A. Wood, *The Russian Revolution* (Longman, 1979), p. 80.
10 A. Marwick ed., *Total War and Social Change* (Macmillan, 1988), p. xv.
11 M. Kitchen, *The Silent Dictatorship* (London, 1976).
12 I. Porter, and I. Armour, *Imperial Germany 1890–1918* (Longman, 1991), p. 55.
13 H. Strachan ed., *The Oxford Illustrated History of the First World War* (Oxford, 1998), p. 288.

Summary Diagram
The First World War as the First Total War

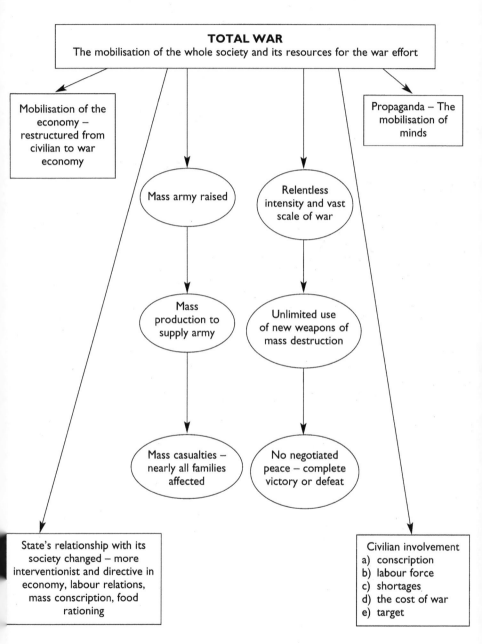

Answering essay questions on Chapter 5

The First World War is a very common subject on exam papers. Typical essay questions are:

1. Why was the First World War so destructive of human life?
2. How far does the First World War represent a fundamental change in the nature of warfare in the period 1792–1918?
3. Was the First World War the first 'Total War'?
4. Do the commanders of the First World War deserve their reputation as 'Butchers and Bunglers'?

For Question 1, start with the obvious:

a) The sheer scale of the war:
   i) Size of the armies, these ran into tens of millions. The more people there were fighting, the greater the number of casualties.
   ii) With the involvement of the British and French worldwide empires and the United States the war was truly a world war.
   iii) Length of the war.
b) The intensity of the fighting. Battles raged with ferocious intensity for months at a time.
c) The highly destructive tactics used:
   i) Mass opening offensives and frontal attacks.
   ii) Attrition – Verdun and the Somme.
   iii) Deliberate targeting of the civilian – blockade, bombing.
d) More deadly weapons used – modern artillery and rifles, machine guns, aeroplanes, submarines, gas, tanks.
e) Finally, you should also bring in the militaristic attitudes and beliefs of the peoples of Europe and their leaders, which meant that they were ready and willing to go to war, and to continue with the war, no matter what the cost.

Question 2 requires an assessment of the First World War in the context of the evolution of warfare from 1792 to 1918. You must demonstrate an awareness of the features of warfare in the periods preceding 1914, i.e. the French Wars 1792–1815 and the development of warfare throughout the nineteenth century. The First World War does represent a significant number of changes in the nature of warfare and these are summarised in the introduction to this chapter. Remember that the essay title opens with the phrase 'How far does . . .' and this is asking you to present both those areas of change and those areas of continuity.

For the information required for essay 3, see the summary diagram on page 101.

For question 4, see the information in the section on Leadership. Provide a balanced account by outlining the case against the leaders and then their defence. Refer to the leading critics of the generals as well as their defenders.

Source-based question on Chapter 5

I Study the extract from von Kühlmann's telegram, 3 December 1917, on pages 94–95, the *Punch* cartoon from December 1917, on page 95, and the British propaganda poster on page 92.

a) What was the purpose behind each of these examples of the use of propaganda? *(10 marks)*

b) How helpful are these sources in demonstrating the different strategies and techniques of the propaganda war? *(10 marks)*

c) Using these examples, and any others you are aware of, assess the impact of propaganda in the First World War. *(20 marks)*

The Second World War

POINTS TO CONSIDER

World War Two followed only 20 years after World War One and therefore there were many similarities in the characteristics of warfare between the two conflicts. Yet there were also significant differences between the two. As you read through the chapter you need to build up a firm understanding of those similarities and differences.

KEY DATES

1939	**September**	Outbreak of the war in Europe.
		Success of German blitzkrieg attacks – the Fall of France.
1940		The Battle of Britain.
1941	**June**	The invasion of the Soviet Union.
1941	**December**	Japanese attack on Pearl Harbour – USA enters the war.
1943	**February**	German defeat at Stalingrad – Russia on the offensive.
1944	**June**	Western Allies invade France (D-Day).
1945	**May**	Germany surrenders.
1945	**August**	Two atomic bombs dropped on Japan – Japanese surrender.

1 Introduction

> **KEY ISSUE** What was the relationship between the First World War and the Second World War?

World War One and World War Two are inextricably linked. Many writers, inspired by Foch's despairing remark in 1919, have termed the period 1919–1939 'the twenty years' truce' and portrayed the Second World War as Hitler's attempt to settle unfinished business from 1918. The unprecedented devastation and suffering of World War One certainly led to the rise of revisionist states and anti-democratic leaders determined to overturn the peace settlement. It also shattered the alliance that had finally defeated Germany in 1918. The USA retreated into isolationism, Russia became the communist USSR and considered all capitalist states bitter enemies, France had been traumatised and weakened, and Britain had been severely weakened economically. Germany was therefore confronted by a ring of small, newly-created states and divided great powers.

Strategically Germany was in a stronger position in 1939 than it had been in 1914.

The First World War also shaped the Second World War in other ways. The First World War was the formative military experience of the politicians, generals and strategists who were in command from 1939 to 1945. Their judgements on tactics and strategy were based on the differing lessons they drew from 1914–18 and the weapons they were to fight with were largely improved versions of the weapons they had used in the earlier conflict.

2 Tactical Breakthrough: Blitzkrieg

KEY ISSUE How did blitzkrieg reintroduce mobility to warfare?

Between 1939 and 1941 Hitler's armies achieved what had been considered impossible for the majority of World War One, that is, quick, decisive victories with relatively little cost to manpower and resources. During this time Poland was defeated in less than a month, Denmark and Norway in two months, Holland in five days, Belgium in 17 days, Yugoslavia in 11 days, and Greece in three weeks. Hitler's greatest prize during this dramatic period was the defeat of France in six weeks and the driving of British troops from the continent. By the end of 1941 Hitler's armies had struck eastwards against their ideological enemy the Soviet Union; they were within sight of Moscow and had killed or captured nearly 5 million Soviet troops. These astounding victories were due to a new form of co-ordinated warfare that became known as blitzkrieg ('lightning war').

a) The Technology of Blitzkrieg

Blitzkrieg was a return to mobility in land warfare that had been so absent for most of World War One. Yet the technology that made blitzkrieg possible – the tank, the motor vehicle, and the aeroplane – had been available in World War One. Now it was their greater reliability, range and power, plus an understanding of their combined use, that made blitzkrieg attacks so devastating and effective. The dominant battleground features of World War One – the machine gun, barbed wire, fixed artillery and trenches – gave the upper hand to the defensive. But by 1939 the technological balance of power had tilted towards the attacker. The essence of blitzkrieg was surprise, speed and movement – the core elements of Napoleonic warfare now enhanced by modern technology. It involved the co-ordinated use of all available forces striking at the enemy's weakest point, not as in World War One spread over a very long front. The first surprise attack was designed to take out the enemy's headquarters, communications and air force on the ground by air strike or long range artillery.

Parachutists were dropped behind enemy lines, and massed tanks and armoured cars – supported by fighter and bomber planes – cut through the enemy defences. Armoured cars and lorries then rapidly delivered infantry reinforcements to exploit the breakthrough. Communication and co-ordination between units was made possible by radio contact now installed in planes, tanks and troop transporters. Once this breakthrough had been achieved, the infantry and artillery were used to secure and hold the position. A large part of the effectiveness of blitzkrieg was the panic and confusion produced by this unimagined mobility and advance. Opponents became quickly demoralised and surrendered rapidly. These tactics were a dangerous gamble in that they were open to counter-attack, and their advance forces might become overextended and isolated. It was only Germany that sought to use the opportunity provided by the more effective technology of 1939. For them the gamble paid off in dramatic fashion until 1942.

b) Why Germany Adopts Blitzkrieg

That Germany alone in Europe took up the option of blitzkrieg was due to the lessons the Germans drew from World War One, their state of military preparation and the nature of their leadership. Germany had learnt from the last desperate attacks of 1918 (the Ludendorff offensive) that surprise, concentrated attacks by storm troops, and tactical air cover could break the defensive deadlock. During the inter-war period a number of strategists, principally in Britain and France but also Guderian in Germany, had advanced the theories of rapid mobile attack based upon concentrations of tanks. Crucially it was the German leadership that put this theory into practice. As the speed, mobility and reliability of tanks improved, the more feasible their role as the cutting edge of the new offensive warfare became.

The risky tactics of blitzkrieg appealed to Hitler's gambler instincts and he personally pushed the build-up of these units and insisted on their use in 1939–40, often against the caution of his generals. Another appeal of blitzkrieg for Hitler was that it was a cheap option (if it succeeded) in terms of resources and casualties. The wars in Europe had come earlier than Hitler had anticipated. He did not expect the Polish invasion to lead to European war and his long term preparations for the ultimate struggle for world power would not be complete until 1943–5. Blitzkrieg offered the possibility of short decisive victories before Germany became the economic and military superpower that Hitler had planned for. Wars would be over in weeks, and Germany would not be dragged into another grinding war of attrition that broke her in 1918. The speed of victories delivered by blitzkrieg would prevent the full mobilisation of economies and societies against Germany. Another reason for the adoption and success of blitzkrieg was that it was the weapon of the country most prepared for war, mentally and physically. Hitler had conditioned his people, his economy and his military for war from the moment he came to power. His opponents were divided, fearful and unprepared for the sudden horrific onslaught.

c) The Success of Blitzkrieg

The success of blitzkrieg was not a matter of superior numbers, in terms of either manpower or weapons. This may have been the case in Poland in September 1939, but not in France in 1940 where the forces were approximately equal, or Russia in 1941 where the balance favoured the Soviets. The French and British had more tanks than Germany but fewer of them were concentrated in tank or mobile armoured divisions. They were hampered by a defensive doctrine that would not risk them without artillery cover and many of them were dispersed among the infantry. The German tanks and armoured cars were concentrated in mass in advance shock units. They sought to achieve breakthrough at the weakest point, race ahead and allow Germany's second, slower wave of attackers to consolidate and hold the ground. In fact Germany had virtually two armies: only a relatively small proportion were tank or full motorised divisions, the rest were indistinguishable from their 1914 predecessors dependent on railway transportation, horses or marching. Therefore the elite Panzer tank divisions, although only ten per cent of the army, bore a heavy responsibility in achieving victory. The one clear area of superiority for Germany in 1940 was in the air, where she had more modern aircraft and a 3:2 advantage. This advantage was crucial in support of the dramatic German Panzer thrust through the relatively undefended Ardennes forest, and its 250 mile sprint to the coast to cut the Allied forces in two. The Nazi forces owed their breakthrough to surprise and superior organisation and morale.

In the face of the German challenge the Allies were disorganised, slow to respond and unable to co-ordinate their efforts. France and Britain, fearful of a counter-attack, had missed the opportunity to attack when Germany was engaged in Poland. France and Britain were hamstrung by a defensive strategy that envisaged a military re-run of World War One, in which mass offensives would founder on fixed defences. The French had taken great care to construct mighty border defences in the form of the Maginot Line but it became a strategic liability when they were unwilling to fight beyond the protection of the Line. This misplaced reliance on fixed defences in a more mobile age has been called a 'Maginot mentality'.

3 Tactics and Strategy: The Limits of Blitzkrieg and the Allied Response

KEY ISSUE How was blitzkrieg defeated?

a) The Tide Turns

Despite stunning victories in Europe and Russia, which exceeded even Napoleon's conquests, by the end of 1941 a series of events turned the war dramatically against the Axis powers. After heavy losses, the Soviets began to reorganise and launch a ferocious counter-attack. In December 1941 the Japanese attacked the US naval base of Pearl Harbour, causing America to declare war on Japan. Hitler immediately declared war on the US and President Roosevelt was able to break the shackles of isolationism to declare war on Nazi Germany as well. Also Britain (and her empire), after her survival in the Battle of Britain, remained in the war and put increasing pressure on the Axis powers in the Mediterranean and North Africa. But Western pressure needed time to take effect. The US did not have a large standing army or reserves and her civilian economy needed to transform itself to support its own, and its allies', war needs. After that had been achieved the Western allies then faced the most difficult of military tasks – to launch a massive amphibious campaign against a well-defended continent.

In the meantime, the war was to be decided on the Eastern Front. Indeed the scale of the war in the East dwarfed all other fronts. In the West the war was contested by armies of a few dozen divisions; in the east it involved the direct and sustained engagement of several hundred divisions. Between 1941 and 1945 the Red Army destroyed over 600 German and allied divisions.

b) The Breaking of Blitzkrieg in the East

Towards the end of 1941 the German army was confronted with the consequences of the miscalculations of their leadership and the limitations of blitzkrieg. After the success of lightning war in the West, Hitler was convinced that he would achieve the same results in Russia. He was also convinced of his own military infallibility. As a result he underestimated the task before him. As he said at the beginning of the invasion 'We'll kick the door in and the whole rotten building will fall down.' Yet despite committing 4 million German and allied troops to the invasion it was not large enough or sufficiently equipped for the scale and intensity of the operation. Germany committed only slightly more planes and tanks to the invasion of Russia than to the Battle of France. In very short wars over relatively confined areas where opponents surrendered after the opening onslaught, blitzkrieg worked brilliantly. In Russia, however, none of these things applied. Despite massive initial losses Russia did not break, and with her vast reserves of manpower and resources she was able to regroup and re-equip. In traditional fashion Russia was able to trade space for time.

Germany, now facing a possible three-front war, could not afford the time or resources for a long war of attrition. Hitler and his generals had expected the war in the East to last three months and therefore had not planned or equipped for a winter war. In the winter of 1941–2, when temperatures reached minus 40 degrees centigrade, his troops did not even have winter clothing. In the vast distances of the German advance long supply lines were vulnerable to the harsh weather conditions and to counter-attack. German losses in manpower and equipment were huge, Russia's were even greater – but, crucially, it was Russia not Germany that could replace those losses. Forward units of Panzers and armoured vehicles, which raced ahead of the infantry, became isolated and vulnerable, especially without the air supremacy they had enjoyed in the West. Without back-up troops, supplies and air cover, the German cutting-edge tank and armoured divisions no longer looked like war winners. The tactical balance had shifted. If tanks could be used for attack they could equally be used for counter-attack. Anti-tank guns became more effective and more widely produced. Minefields were used to defend against tank break-throughs. In the offensive, mobile artillery was regaining its position of dominance, as demonstrated by the British in North Africa at the third battle of El Alamein in 1942.

Germany had lost the element of surprise crucial to blitzkrieg, and Russian forces, along with the other Allies, could learn from the German example. Just as Napoleon's adversaries had realised that they had to become 'more like the French' to defeat him, so the Allies facing the threat of Nazism had to become militarily more like the Germans. Accordingly the Soviets established new tank armies supported by mobile infantry and its own artillery, all based upon the German Panzer division. The Soviet air force was concentrated into large air armies with fighters and bombers acting together instead of being spread along the front. Russian counter-attacks, such as the one that trapped 200,000 German troops at Stalingrad, became irresistible. The German army's advanced mobile cutting edge was blunted and it became more reliant on horses than mechanised vehicles. Richard Overy describes the 'demodernisation' of the German army from 1941, as 'the losses sustained in combat and from wear saw the modern army crumble away'.[1]

c) The Reversal of Blitzkrieg

By 1944 Germany's tactical and weapons superiority had been reversed, dominance of the skies rested with the Allies in all theatres of the war, and Hitler's leadership, which had delivered such successes from 1939 to 1941, was now a fatal liability. The German army maintained an impressive operational effectiveness, but good tactics without good strategy was a recipe for disaster. The Western Allies' actions in the Mediterranean, North Africa and Italy tied down many German divisions that were desperately needed on the Eastern Front. By the time the Allies launched the D Day landings in Normandy in June 1944 Germany was over-stretched and under-equipped. The danger of the U boat threat had been blunted and the *Luftwaffe* was a pale shadow of its former glory. During the invasion Allied air forces enjoyed a superiority of 70:1. The German forces were in position behind defences (the 'Atlantic Wall'), but now it was their turn to experience a blitzkrieg offensive. There was extensive bombing of communications centres, railways and defensive positions prior to the invasion, as well as a successful deception by the Allies of their intended landing sites. Paratroops were landed hours before the major assault. Within five days over 300,000 Allied troops were on French soil and the full weight of the Allied forces was brought down on Nazi Germany.

4 Leadership

KEY ISSUES How did Hitler prove to be a liability as a war leader? What were the strengths and weaknesses of the Allied leaders?

a) Hitler

Hitler's war leadership was an extension of his domestic leadership style before 1939: it was dictatorial, chaotic and shaped by his ideological and racist prejudices. Hitler held full military and political responsibility for all decisions on war, its timing and its strategy. One of Hitler's enduring military principles was the insistence on the offensive no matter how improbable the likelihood of success. From 1939 to 1941 the gamble paid off, confirming his belief in his military infallibility. From the middle of 1941, however, his leadership became a serious diplomatic and military liability and was one of the major reasons for the defeat of Germany. In 1941 his badly prepared and badly timed invasion of Russia and his declaration of war on the USA following the Japanese attack on Pearl Harbour exposed Germany to the mightiest coalition of forces in history. As blitzkrieg foundered on Russian resistance in 1942–3, Hitler could not re-adjust his tactics. The strengths he brought to the early phase of blitzkrieg – improvisation and daring – became weaknesses as the war became an attritional struggle which required rigorous planning and co-ordinated, realistic strategy. In the words of A.W. Purdue, 'as a commander in a defensive war, he was a disaster'.[2] When Hitler's generals realised that Germany needed to resort to a flexible defence which allowed for strategic withdrawals, Hitler overruled them insisting on no retreats and a fight to the finish. He announced that the war would leave only 'survivors and annihilated'. This order condemned Von Paulus's 200,00 strong 6th Army to a hopeless last-ditch stand at Stalingrad in the winter of 1942–3. As defeat became more certain Hitler retreated into fantasy and a fussy interference in low level operational tactics. Strategy was ignored or discussed not with the generals but close party cronies. Those generals who stood against him he sacked or transferred; his appointments were based primarily on loyalty to him or the party. The most incompetent of these was Göring, who survived as Commander in chief of the German air force despite his failings at Dunkirk, the Battle of Britain and Stalingrad. Hitler's personality and leadership style prevented co-ordination between the military services. With this leadership handicap, it is a testament to the extraordinary fighting ability of the German armed forces that they managed to resist the Allies until 1945.

b) The Allies

In contrast to the disastrous impact that Hitler had upon Germany's war effort, all of the Allies' leaders, despite certain defects, made a genuine contribution to their nation's victory. They achieved genuine strategic, economic and intelligence co-operation which significantly maximised the collective power of their alliance.

i) Churchill

Churchill was the only wartime leader who was specifically appointed as a war leader. His pugnacity, his implacable opposition to appeasement, and his wartime experience made him the only realistic alternative after the resignation of Chamberlain. In fact in both world wars Churchill's strategic interventions have drawn severe criticism. In 1915 he was responsible for the disastrous Gallipoli campaign and in 1940 he promoted the badly organised Norwegian invasion. 1941–2 saw further setbacks for his ventures in Greece, Crete and Singapore. Like Hitler, Churchill always favoured the offensive especially if it seemed to offer a dramatic 'quick fix' delivered by naval or air power. He was a constant meddler in strategic matters, but he would not overrule his Chiefs of Staff and his experienced generals learned to stand up to him. Churchill's contribution was not strategic; it was primarily in terms of morale. In the dark days of 1940, after the fall of France and when survival, let alone victory, was far from certain, Churchill's personal defiance, expressed brilliantly in speeches and radio broadcasts, stiffened the nation's defiance and determination. Churchill's other significant contribution to the Allied war effort was his statesmanship and effort in establishing and maintaining the Grand Alliance.

ii) Roosevelt

Franklin D. Roosevelt alone among the wartime leaders made no pretence at being a strategist. However, the general commitments he gave to support Britain and the USSR, and the policy of defeating Germany before Japan, shaped the course and outcome of the war. Roosevelt declared that he was going to take a greater role in the conduct of the war than his World War One predecessor, Woodrow Wilson. Yet once the structures for the organisation of the war were established Roosevelt was content to receive reports from them. In fact one of the weaknesses of Roosevelt's leadership was his informal approach to meetings and decision-making that left a number of his subordinates unclear on what his actual policies were. Roosevelt's major achievement was to provide inspirational, steadfast leadership achieved through a spirit of conciliation. Roosevelt also believed, like Churchill but with greater justification, that he was responsible for keeping a rather mismatched Alliance together.

iii) Stalin

Stalin's leadership demonstrated the strengths and weaknesses of his position as absolute dictator of the Soviet Union. He had centralised all power, political and military, in himself. This had nearly cost Russia the war in the opening Nazi onslaught when Stalin was so shocked by the attack that he was frozen into complete inactivity. There were no alternative leaders as Stalin had spent the previous 15 years exterminating them and for weeks Russia remained leaderless as blitzkrieg raged. Stalin had actually made the Soviet task more daunting by his purge of the Red Army leadership in 1937–8 when more than two-thirds of the country's senior commanders were imprisoned or shot. Remarkably Russia survived these self-inflicted wounds and Stalin played a significant part in the defeat of Germany.

Fortunately for Russia and the Allies, Stalin, unlike Hitler, was at least aware of his limitations as a commander, and he appointed Georgii Zhukov as his deputy. It was an inspired choice. Zhukov proved to be the greatest commander of the Second World War. Stalin also rolled back the oppressive control of the communist party commissars over the army, thereby increasing both the effectiveness and morale of the armed forces. Planners, managers and bureaucrats were similarly freed from political interference and war production expanded rapidly. Stalin still exercised close personal supervision over the conduct of the war, but like his Alliance counterparts he increasingly accepted the professional authority of his commanders and managers. One of his greatest contributions was motivation. He was able to draw upon the personal stature he had built up in creating a near god-like 'personality cult' during the 1930s. He acted as a focus for national loyalty and resistance. With this appeal, backed up by terror, he was able to secure almost super-human efforts and sacrifices from the Soviet people.

5 The Air War

> **KEY ISSUE** What was the impact of the Allies' strategic bombing offensive?

The First World War had revealed the potential of air power, but the major powers drew sharply differing conclusions about its role in the next conflict. Britain placed great faith in the power of the bomber as an offensive force against an enemy population. The two targets of this 'strategic' bombing would be the enemy economy and civilian morale. Bombing was to be the primary agent of total war. In fact Britain placed so much faith in an air war that some advocates of this approach suggested that it would remove the need for infantry attack. The air force in a short but horrific bombing offensive would be a war winner on its own. Only the US shared this faith in the effectiveness of long-range strategic bombing. Germany, Russia and France drew different lessons from the First World War, and then from the Spanish Civil War, and concluded that the primary role of the air force was 'tactical' – at the front in support of their armies. Blitzkrieg appeared to confirm the value of an air force fully integrated into a combined military operation. The successes of blitzkrieg would not have been possible without the *Luftwaffe's* early bombing raids and air cover for tank and infantry attacks. In this way aircraft transformed land warfare and consigned the stalemate of trench warfare to history.

After British land forces were driven from the continent during the fall of France, the only practical way that Britain could strike against Germany was by bombing the German homeland. Yet these early raids were ineffective and produced unsustainable losses of aircraft and crew, especially since Germany was defended by 50,000 anti-air-craft guns and experienced fighter pilots. The widely held belief of the 1930s that 'the bomber will always get through' was disproved by hard reality. Technically the raids were impractical without further technological improvements in navigation, bomb aiming and long-range fighter escort. In 1941 it was calculated that at best only one aircraft in three got within five miles of its target.

Yet by 1943 many of these technological improvements were in place and, as a substitute for a second front in France, Churchill and Roosevelt gave priority to the bombing campaign when they met at Casablanca. The intensification of the bombing offensive in 1943, however, had only limited results and incurred disastrous losses. This produced a change of strategy by the Allies. With the Allied invasion of Europe planned for late spring 1944, the Western forces had to achieve air supremacy or the entire D Day operation would be in jeopardy. The Allies concluded that nothing less than the destruction of the German air force would achieve this. On 1st January 1944 the Commander in Chief of the American air forces issued the instruction to 'Destroy the enemy air force wherever you find them in the air, on the ground and in the factories'.[3]

The new strategy put more emphasis on increasing the effectiveness of the fighter escorts. The single most effective device in this area was remarkably simple and 'low tech': it was the fitting of disposable fuel tanks on to Allied fighter planes. This immediately increased the range of the fighter escorts from 500 to 2,000 miles and transformed the balance of power over the skies of Germany. The superiority of Allied aircraft production was now used to devastating effect. By the winter of 1944–5 Germany lost nearly one-quarter of its fighters every month; by the spring these losses had risen to half their fighter force each month. The *Luftwaffe* was systematically taken apart and with it Germany's entire war effort. Germany was exposed to the full force of the Allied bombing offensive and her war economy was shattered. Industry and communications were worn down and disrupted, oil production was reduced to a trickle and 9,000 aircraft were destroyed on the ground. It was a blockade imposed from the skies. The indirect effect of the bombing offensive was equally as damaging. German anti-aircraft defences sucked in over 2 million men who were desperately needed at the front. Fighter aircraft were withdrawn from the Eastern Front and France for the protection of Germany. In the last year of war the effects of destruction by bombing and the diversion of men, aircraft and supplies robbed German forces of half of their battle front weapons and equipment. By April 1944 Soviet forces had an air superiority of 26:1. Allied air superiority was crucial in the invasion of Europe in June 1944. Preparatory bombing raids were made in Germany and France to disrupt transport and railway networks and prevent the movement of supplies and reinforcements to Normandy. In the air the Western Allies had a massive superiority of 70:1.

In the Far East American bombing of the Japanese mainland had an even more decisive impact than that on Germany. By the spring of 1945, after hard fighting, the Americans had overrun the outlying Japanese islands from which they could launch virtually unopposed air raids. The raids devastated the undefended cities of houses constructed of wood and paper. Uncontrollable firestorms produced 8 million refugees. Even at this stage Japan's military leadership defied their emperor and refused to surrender until two atomic bombs destroyed the cities of Hiroshima and Nagasaki. American troops had been spared the deadly task of invasion and air power alone forced the Japanese surrender.

The strategic bombing offensive was one of the most controversial features of the Second World War. It was one of the central features of total war as it deliberately targeted civilians with the aim of breaking enemy morale. With the restricted technology of the period even those raids against economic or military targets were so inaccurate that civilians were again the main victims. As John Buckley writes, 'In

The destruction of Dresden, 1945. One of the most controversial targets of strategic bombing.

many ways air war was the epitome of total war.'[4] The air offensive could not deliver victory by itself, as early advocates had argued, but it was a powerful weapon in weakening war production and German resistance on all fronts. In Italy the unopposed bombing campaign of 1943 brought about the fall of Mussolini and the Italian surrender. In Japan in 1945 it secured the Japanese surrender and by removing the need for invasion saved many thousands of American and probably millions of Japanese lives.

6 Resources and Economic Warfare

> **KEY ISSUE** How did the Allies win the economic war?

As we have seen in previous chapters, the balance of resources ('the sinews of war') played a vital role in warfare. Some writers maintain that it was the single most decisive factor in determining the outcome of the Second World War. R.A.C. Parker speaks for many when he claims: 'Superior resources won the war: the victors had greater numbers of men and women and made more weapons'.[5] But against this we must remember that, vital as resources are, wars are not settled purely by an economic balance sheet. Leadership, weapons technology, fighting ability and sheer chance all play their part.

a) Germany

For Hitler, the lessons of Germany's economic unpreparedness and collapse in the First World War were not to be repeated. In 1936 the Führer decreed that the German economy and military should prepare for war in a four year plan. Between 1936 and 1939 over two-thirds of all German industrial investment went into war-related projects. Mostly this was on weapons spending, but Hitler was acutely aware of Germany's shortage of war materials in World War One. Oil supplies were a particular problem: on the eve of war the Axis powers controlled only three per cent of the world's oil resources. In response to this Germany became the world leader in the production of synthetic oil produced from coal. No country in peacetime had ever prepared so rigorously for war. Yet in the first three years of war the German economy under-achieved, relative to its position of dominance and conquest during this period. Up until 1943 the smaller British economy out-produced the newly expanded Reich in almost all classes of weapon. This was largely due to the inefficiency and confusion of rival German agencies trying to organise the war effort. Factories and industrial methods were not modernised, and the army rather than heads of industry determined economic production. The result was obstruction, misplaced effort and research, and a chronic inability to harness the massively expanded resources made available by conquest. The military wasted its energies in a vast array of fruitless projects which led to the production of 425 different models of aircraft, 151 different makes of lorry, and 150 different motor-cycles. Some of these designs were inspired but they threw away the vital economic advantage of mass production.

By 1942 Hitler was determined to sweep away the inefficiencies and appointed Albert Speer (his personal architect) as Minister of Armaments. Finally, under Speer's direction, Nazi Germany embarked on a total war effort. Speer was a brilliant organiser and was able to bring efficiency and unity to Germany's war production. His greatest achievement was to take control of production away from the army and make best use of the flexibility and expertise of private industry. The great variety of weapons was reduced to several functional, mass produced models. Weapons production trebled in three years and output per worker doubled. Greater numbers of foreign workers (many of them as slave labour) were drafted in so that by 1944 30 per cent of all industrial workers in Germany were foreign, totalling 9.3 million. Yet despite Speer's efforts the Nazi war effort was hampered by its own destructive ideology which outweighed economic practicalities. Speer wanted the foreign workers better fed and cared for so that they would be more productive, but Nazi racist brutality was not moderated and many of these workers died and nearly all were on starvation rations. Speer was also blocked in his plans to bring more women into the workforce and vital resources were devoted to the extermination of the Jews rather than the war effort. By 1944 the Allied bombing campaign had reduced production of war materials by 40 per cent and oil supplies, the 'Achilles' Heel' of the Axis powers, by 90 per cent. Speer's efforts could not save Germany from its fate.

b) The Allies

i) The Soviet Union
By the end of 1941 the Soviet Union faced disaster; their loss of men, territory and resources was terrifying. The USSR had lost half of its best farmland, three-quarters of its iron, coal and steel and one-third of its electricity and rail network. Yet from 1942 they produced many more high quality tanks, guns and aircraft than the Germans. This remarkable recovery was achieved by the wholesale removal of factories (some 2,600) which were reassembled in the East beyond the reach of the Germans, in the Urals, Siberia and Kazakhstan, taking with them millions of refugees and workers. One survivor remembered, 'It was as if the world was tilted up. Everything human and mechanical was moved East.' In addition, 2,300 new factories were built in 1942–44. Strict regimentation and discipline of the workforce was imposed; two-thirds of the female population were conscripted for war work, enduring harsh discipline and long working hours. The

output of the Soviet worker increased nearly three-fold during the course of the war. Prisoners in labour camps were mercilessly absorbed into the war effort with rations provided only for those who worked. The result was a war economy more fully mobilised and disciplined than any other country, 'a single war camp' as Stalin called it. Western aid also played a significant part in the form of raw materials, equipment and food rather than weapons. This provided half of Soviet explosives and aircraft fuel, half a million US vehicles and 1,900 American trains, while the Soviets produced just 92. Britain and the US supplied 35,000 radio stations and 625,000 field telephones under lend-lease bringing about a communications revolution.

The vital factor in the Russians' economic mobilisation was not a basic superiority of resources; but compared with the Germans, the Soviets made far better use of the resources they did have. The total control that Stalin's regime had built up in the 1930s, the almost superhuman sacrifice and effort of her people, and a highly effective planned command economy – these were the crucial elements in the Soviet Union's survival and eventual victory. By 1943 Russia had transformed its economic war effort so that they had twice as many troops and four times as many tanks as the Germans.

ii) The United States
In December 1940 President Roosevelt had pledged that the US would act as 'the arsenal of democracy', a promise which resulted in vital supplies to Britain via the lend-lease scheme. Valuable as these resources were in 1941 they were dwarfed by America's later economic contribution to the Allied war effort once her civilian economy was adapted for war production. As a direct contrast to the Soviet model, this transformation was achieved with the voluntary co-operation of private industry. Capitalism went to war for America. The Americans relied on the proven strengths of their capitalist economy – its quicksilver flexibility, technical know-how, and vast mass production techniques.

The advanced American car industry with its mechanisation and mass production line methods became the powerhouse of the American war effort. Tanks, planes and ships all rolled off the same production line which had previously produced cars. General Motors alone produced 10 per cent of all American war production. The Ford company produced more military equipment during the war than Italy. In total the American economy produced almost two-thirds of all the Allied military equipment manufactured in the war. From as early as 1942 the US out-produced the weapons output of all of the Axis powers combined.

iii) Britain
In many ways Britain achieved an impressive social and economic mobilisation. Partly this was due to the successful experience of World

War One, the increasing acceptance of government intervention, and the desperate situation Britain found itself in. Again the mines, shipping and the railways came under state control. Rationing was introduced and labour, both male and female, was increasingly mobilised. The costs of war were met by high taxation, the sale of assets to the US, aid from the Commonwealth and the vital lend-lease scheme with America. Yet Britain's weapons output was mixed. The British reached the limit of their war potential relatively early in the war, out-producing Germany in most weapons up to 1942. Thereafter production in aircraft continued to outpace Germany's until 1944, but Britain could not match Germany for tanks and other weapons as Germany approached her full potential. The British war effort reflected a number of the weaknesses evident in her industry in the 1930s such as poor design, low productivity and limited mechanisation. By the end of 1943 Britain had reached its limit. Unlike Germany it could not make use of conquered territories and peoples, and unlike the USSR it could not compel its own citizens. The British war effort depended on collective determination and the willingness of her people to make voluntary sacrifices. It achieved these in high measure.

7 Science and Technology at War

> **KEY ISSUE** Why did the Allies develop a lead in the field of science and technology?

All participants in World War Two realised that the sophistication and technological effectiveness of their weapons, communications and detection systems were crucial. A technological arms race developed to gain a tactical advantage and then to continually refine the product to maintain that advantage.

The technological race was more evident in the air and at sea rather than in the land war. On land the war was won with improved versions of the weapons of the First World War: tanks, trucks, aircraft, and artillery. The Allies managed to improve their versions of these weapons, while the Axis powers did not, and nor could they match the sheer quantity of Allied production. Japanese weapons were outdated and military transport inadequate; Italy's industrial base was not developed enough to make a useful contribution to the Axis cause. Germany, however, had an excellent engineering and science base. Germans pioneered the weapons of the later Cold War (jets, rockets and atomic weapons); but during the war they were handicapped by political and military interference leading to resources being wasted on far too many prototypes and projects. Only a fraction of its army, the cutting edge, was equipped with technically advanced equipment. Once that cutting edge had been blunted in Russia, and Germany ran short of resources, her forces technologically went backwards. By 1944 only one tenth of Germany's army was mechanised.

At sea new weapons were developed such as more sophisticated German mines, which quickly led to more sophisticated anti-mine devices in reply. The most important area of research for the Allies was in the detection of U-boats. This led to more effective sonar and radar to pinpoint the location of submarines. Radar, a pre-war British development, played a vital role in the air and sea war. It was crucial in the defence of Britain during the Battle of Britain and in detecting U-boats from the air in the Battle of the Atlantic. Germany also had advanced radar equipment but, anticipating a short war, they had not developed it properly. The Allies were further aided in the anticipation of German movements by the British breaking of the German codes, using the first digital computer. Also, in what was called the Battle of the Beams, radio beams were used to guide bombers to their targets until defenders blocked the threat by jamming the signals. The Allies then developed further navigational aids in 1942 to improve targeting, which proved essential for night raids. The most sophisticated of these was the H_2S, a radar transmitter and receiver fitted in the bomber.

The air war consisted of a continuous process of innovation and counter innovation in navigational and targeting aids, radio and radar jamming devices and the design of aircraft. By 1943 the allies were gaining the upper hand. The new generation of American bombers (the Flying Fortress and the Liberator) and long range fighters (the Thunderbolt, the Mustang and the Lightning) gave the Allies a superiority in quality as well as quantity. At the same time on the Eastern Front the Soviets had managed to match the Germans in the quality of their aircraft and to massively out-produce them. The German response was in a pilotless flying bomb, the V1, and the armed rocket, the V2. Hitler supported the expensive development of rocket technology due to the failure of his conventional weapons and it fitted in with his fantasies of a 'wonder weapon' that would turn the tide of war. Although targeted at London the V1s and V2s were not war winners. They could not be mass-produced, they were unreliable and inaccurate and they were overrun by invading Allied forces before they could have a significant impact. On balance they had a deleterious effect on the German war effort as the rocket programme consumed vast funds which could have produced an estimated 24,000 fighter planes, or been used in other projects. For example the Germans had developed the first ground-to-air missile which had demonstrated its potential against enemy bombers, but it was starved of resources and backing.

The most outstanding example of science and technology producing a 'wonder weapon' was the atomic bomb. This, like nearly all the weapons and detection systems introduced during the Second World War, was based upon pre-war discoveries and developments. The war and the dread of Germany developing the first such bomb provided the motivation for the vast investment and concentrated scientific effort to develop the weapon. It was only America that had the economic and scientific resources and a supportive leadership to undertake this task. Even then the vast American effort, the Manhattan Project, only produced a weapon for use after the German surrender. Germany did not have the economic resources for such a programme, and the menace of the Nazi regime had driven many invaluable scientists out of Europe and into the arms of the Allies. Perhaps most decisive was the lack of political backing, as Hitler and other Nazi leaders viewed the project as ideologically unacceptable as it was based on Einstein's theories and therefore condemned as non-Aryan 'Jewish science'. The atomic bomb was not a war winner even in the Far East, but it was a final blow against an already defeated enemy.

8 Public Opinion, Morale and Propaganda

> **KEY ISSUE** Why was there no noticeable collapse of morale on the home front?

One of the enduring legacies of the First World War was the assumption that propaganda would play a crucial role in the next war. Total war demanded total commitment. Morale, for both soldiers and civilians, was seen as a vital factor in a nation's military effort. The mutinies in the French armies in 1917, the revolutions in Russia in the same year, and the collapse of the home front in Germany and Austria-Hungary in late 1918 all appeared to offer clear demonstrations of the dangers of the breakdown of morale. The basic military objectives of propaganda were to reinforce morale at home and to sow dissension and defeatism in the enemy.

a) Allied Public Opinion and Propaganda

As war approached the Allied democracies were at a distinct disadvantage. The dictators that faced them had established well-oiled propaganda machines that for years had shaped their people for war. In contrast, Britain and the USA were open societies in which pacifism and isolationism dominated the public mood. This pacifism arose as a revulsion against the loss and suffering of World War One and the fear of the next war, made more terrifying by the use of even more destructive weapons in the form of air raids and gas attacks targeted at civilians. For both Britain and America the rapid turnaround in public opinion was achieved not by their own propaganda but by the actions of the dictators. In Britain the war scare of the Munich crisis in September 1938 confronted the British public and government with the very real threat presented by Hitler and his allies. From this time onward rapid rearmament and a hardening of public opinion went hand in hand. At the outbreak of war the populations of Britain and France, and their empires, answered the call to arms as conscientiously as their 1914 predecessors, though the earlier wild enthusiasm was now replaced by grim but resolute determination. In the US a 1939 opinion poll revealed 99 per cent support for isolationism. It was only the harsh reality of the Japanese attack on Pearl Harbour and Hitler's declaration of war that shattered the hopes of the isolationists.

Cartoon from the *Daily Mail*, 18 February 1942, three days after the embarrassing British surrender to the Japanese at Singapore. The message given is that this is only a temporary setback against a backward ape-like race.

Britain's initial propaganda message was largely misjudged and ineffective. Her efforts, such as the RAF 'leaflet raids' on Germany condemning the Nazi invasion of Poland, appeared high-handed and ineffective demands for Germany to mend her ways. The appointment of Winston Churchill as Prime Minister on 10 May 1940 transformed the situation. Churchill immediately set the right tone. He was defiant, pugnacious and brought to his speeches a sense of historic destiny. At the same time the formation of the Political Warfare Executive replaced several competing propaganda agencies. These changes led to a more focused and effective effort based more upon radio than print and aimed against the Nazi leadership not the German people. Radio, now capable of transmission over vast distances, took centre stage in the propaganda war. The British believed that a reputation for reliability would achieve greater results than the more obvious misinformation of Germany. As the Director-General of the BBC, Sir John Reith, proclaimed: 'News is the shocktroops of propaganda'.[6] This tactic proved remarkably successful. As German broadcasts became more boastful but less credible, millions of listeners across occupied Europe risked their lives to tune in to reliable BBC reports. This not only kept up morale in occupied countries by acting as a counterweight to Nazi propaganda but was also used to encourage and organise (in code) resistance movements.

British and American propaganda against the Japanese was markedly different from their efforts directed against Germany. Anti-Nazi propaganda drew a distinction between the Nazi leaders and the German people. It was hoped that pointing out the dangerous and barbarous actions of the Nazi leaders would lead to a break between the people and their rulers. In fact this proved quite fruitless for the duration of the war. Propaganda directed at the Japanese, however, was openly racist and aimed not just at the leadership but at a whole people. In cartoons, for instance, they were portrayed as apes. The official line was that the Japanese were a barbaric, treacherous and fanatical race beyond the civilisation of Europe.

b) The Effect of Propaganda

Despite the efforts of Allied propaganda there was no collapse of morale in Germany or Japan. In Germany the unique popularity of Hitler, and the effectiveness of Goebbels' Ministry of Propaganda, ensured a united front at least until the defeats and bombing raids of 1943. After that point, as Martin Kitchen informs us, 'The Allied bomber offensive, contrary to accepted wisdom, had a shattering effect on civilian morale.'[7] Yet civilian alarm found little outlet, for two reasons. First, the Nazi terror machine was used to quash any potential opposition. In 1942 100,000 Germans were held in concentration camps; by 1945 this figure had reached 500,000. Secondly, and more importantly, the Germans feared the enemy. Goebbels brilliantly played upon this fear and presented Germany's plight as a last ditch defence of 'civilised' Europe from the barbarous Communist and Slavic hordes.

Similar factors operated in Russia. Germany's racist brutality in the USSR was a tactical and propaganda disaster for the Nazis. Potential collaborators, of whom there were millions in the Soviet Union, were effectively driven back into the arms of Stalin. Wisely Stalin acknowledged the limited appeal of a defence of the communist state which had terrorised so many of its own people. The war was recast as the 'Great Patriotic War' to defend not the Soviet Union but 'Mother Russia'. Even Christianity, which had previously been ruthlessly suppressed, was now allowed to reassert itself so that the Church could help encourage national resistance and even raise money for the struggle.

Despite earlier expectations, propaganda did not break enemy morale. The home fronts endured greater privations and suffering than during World War One yet they held firm. A sophisticated manipulation of public opinion (backed by terror in the dictatorships) and a natural fear of the consequences of defeat ensured there would be no internal collapse as had happened in 1917–18.

9 Civilians in the War

> **KEY ISSUE** Why was there greater civilian involvement in the Second World War than in the First World War?

The First World War has been described as total war because of the blurring of the distinction between soldiers and civilians. A large proportion of the civilian populations were mobilised into the war effort and indirectly suffered the effects of war in terms of rationing and deprivation. However, during that conflict it was overwhelmingly the armed forces that did most of the fighting and most of the dying. In the Second World War the balance changed profoundly. In World War One civilians accounted for one-twentieth of the war dead; in the Second World War they were more than half of all deaths. The intensive development of military technology meant that civilians were now drawn into the net of war on a far greater scale. Technology made possible a war of such mobility and reach that tens of millions of people could fall into the hands of their enemies in a matter of weeks. Military technology also allowed vast bombing raids on cities. Technology may have made these things possible but it was the ideological and racial intensity of the conflict, lacking in World War One, which resulted in the use of these technologies with full force against civilian populations.

Civilian casualties were no longer by-products of war: they were now often the direct aims of war. In bombing raids Britain lost 60,000 civilian lives, Germany and Japan nearly 400,000 each; but these figures are overwhelmed by the deliberate destruction of entire peoples who fell into the hands of their enemy. This was most evident on the eastern Front following the German invasion of Poland and the Soviet Union. Here was unleashed what Göring called 'the war of races'. Nazi racist ideology saw their prime enemies as the Jews and the Slavs of Poland and Russia (the so-called 'sub-humans'). Hitler instructed his military commanders that this was to be a war of annihilation. The leader of the SS, Himmler, planned for the slaughter of 30 million Slavs in Western Russia and the Ukraine to make way for the Greater German Reich. Those that were allowed to live were to act as slaves for the master race. Apart from those killed in the fighting there was a greater number who died as a result of starvation, overwork in prisoner of war camps, forced labour or from systematic extermination. Following in the wake of the German invasion of Russia were the SS special 'action squads' with orders to kill all Jews, communist officials and resisters. Although hundreds of thousands were killed in this way the German advance into Russia resulted in far more 'sub-human' civilians falling into their grasp than could be murdered by the traditional methods of bullets and beatings. Forced emigration was not an option due to blockade and so the Nazis resorted to industrialised mass extermination: the 'Final Solution' of the 'Jewish problem'.

The war in the East had removed all moral restraints for the Nazis and provided a perfect cover for their actions. The persecution of the Jews could now descend into mass slaughter. Millions of Jews were transported from across Europe to extermination camps constructed in Poland to be eliminated by poison gas. The camp at Auschwitz-Birkenau alone could dispatch 10,000 a day by this method. With remorseless thoroughness the victims had their possessions, including their spectacles, their gold fillings and even their hair, removed for the German war effort. This was a return to an ancient barbarism in war not witnessed in the modern age, a revival of absolute war made so much more destructive by modern technology. The genocide of the Jews, and the gypsies, was not as a result of enemy action in war: it was the planned, systematic destruction of entire civilian populations.

10 Casualties

KEY ISSUE Which countries suffer the greatest loss of life in the war?

The greater involvement of the civilian in the Second World War is reflected in the grim casualty figures. The Second World War brought about the deaths of 55 million people, nearly five times as many as in the First World War. By far the majority of these occurred in the East and the Far East.

The Soviet Union alone suffered 20 million deaths; 6–7 million were servicemen and women killed in action, a further 2 million in prisoner of war camps, and the remaining 11–12 million were civilian victims. Poland suffered the greatest proportional loss of life with 6 million deaths (3 million of them Jews) out of a total population of 30 million. Only 150,000 of these were killed in military action. Germany lost over 4 million, overwhelmingly servicemen killed on the Eastern Front and in prisoner of war camps. Germany suffered 500,000 civilian losses, with 150,000 German Jews also killed. However, we can also add another 3 million to these figures (nearly all civilians) by including the deaths of Germans living outside the German frontiers of 1937 who were incorporated into the Reich. When defeat came, they were attacked and deported by vengeful native populations.

Britain, France and Italy all suffered fewer losses than in the First World War. For Britain this was 450,000 with a further 120,000 from the empire and dominions. France lost 250,000 in battle but another 350,000 civilians through bombing, reprisals or forced labour; Italy lost 400,000. Yugoslavia, where there was a fierce and divided resistance and brutal reprisals, lost 1.5 million, mostly civilians. An estimated 1 million gypsies and 6 million Jewish civilians were killed in the Nazis' racial extermination programme.

Outside Europe the death toll was equally horrendous. The United States suffered 300,000 war deaths. Japan lost 2.4 million and the Chinese, who were seen as 'inferiors' by the Japanese and from 1937 were treated as ruthlessly as the Nazis dealt with the Slavs, lost an estimated 10 million, nearly all civilians. The death toll in the Far East alone exceeded the death toll on all fronts in the First World War.

11 Conclusion

> **KEY ISSUE** In what ways did the Second World War differ from the First?

The Second World War shared many of the features of the First. Both were world wars with a majority of the world's population formally at war. Both were industrialised wars dependent on the mass production of weapons for mass armies. Both conflicts have been described as total wars. Whole societies and economies were reshaped for the war effort and civilians were thrust into the heart of the struggle as workers and targets. They were both wars of the modern age and lasted long enough for the application of science and technology developed during the wars to affect their outcome. Beyond this, however, there were significant differences between the two wars.

Although both conflicts can be labelled world wars the scale and spread of the Second World War dwarfs that of 1914–18. During the First World War nearly all the significant land fighting took place in

Europe, but the Second World War also involved major theatres of war in North Africa and across Asia. The tactics of the Second World War changed dramatically from the earlier conflict. The dominant military technology, the plane, the tank and motorised transport, had existed in the First World War but they only realised their full potential in the later conflict. This allowed tactics of rapid and devastating mobility and the aerial bombardment of cities. Another area of difference was the impact of ideology in the Second World War that was absent in the first. The First World War had been a struggle of competing nationalisms common to the nineteenth century. The Second World War was driven by the ideologies of Nazi and Japanese racism against communism and democracy. These mutually exclusive ideologies injected a greater intensity to the struggle which engulfed whole populations and ensured a bitter fight to the finish.

The features summarised above, the more destructive weapons and tactics of war, the greater scale of the conflict, the mass industrial production for war, the bitter intensity of the ideological struggle, explain the vast increase in the death toll. The Second World War resulted in five times the number of deaths as those suffered in World War One. It is this extraordinary death toll and the disturbing fact that a majority of these deaths were civilians, mostly killed in cold blood, that provides us with our most enduring impression of World War Two.

References

1   R. Overy, *Why the Allies Won* (Pimlico, 1995), p. 216.
2   A.W. Purdue, *The Second World War* (Macmillan, 1999), p. 150.
3   Overy, *Why the Allies Won,* p. 123.
4   J. Buckley, *Air Power in the Age of Total War* (UCL Press), p. 13.
5   R.A.C. Parker, *The Second World War* (Oxford, 1989), p. 131.
6   P.M. Taylor, *Modern History Review,* Volume 3 No 2, p. 19.
7   M. Kitchen, *Nazi Germany at War* (Longman, 1995), p. 87.

Summary Diagram
Similarities and Differences Between World War One and World War Two

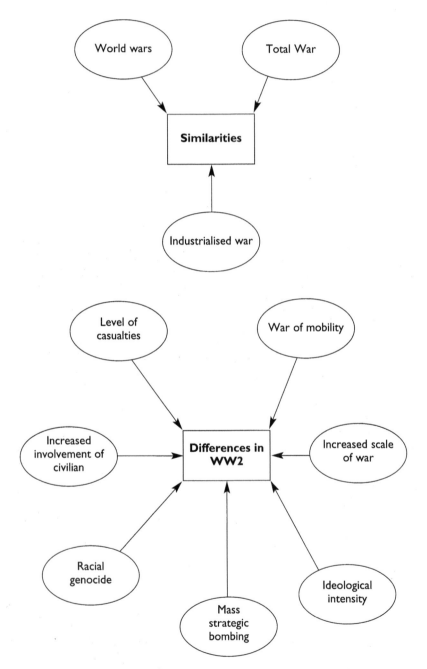

Answering structured and essay questions on Chapter 6

Structured questions are designed to lead you on from a largely descriptive, factual answer to questions that demand a more analytical explanation. For example:

a) How did blitzkrieg achieve such rapid successes for the German army from 1939 to 1941? *(20 marks)*

b) To what extent was the failure of blitzkrieg after 1941 the reason for the defeat of Germany? *(40 marks)*

Note that (2) requires a wider explanation of Germany's defeat than just the reversal of blitzkrieg.

Essay questions on the Second World War appear on many examination papers asking for knowledge on various aspects of the war. Some typical examples are:

1. How far is it true to say that World War Two represents a fundamental change in the nature of warfare compared with World War One?

2. 'Superior resources won the war'. How far do you agree with this judgement on the outcome of World War Two?

3. Why did the Allies win the Second World War?

Question 1 is of a familiar type. 'How far is it true to say . . .' prompts you to provide both sides, i.e. those areas of change and those areas of continuity.

Question 2 picks out one aspect of the conflict and asks you to respond to the quotation by providing a judgement on the relative importance of resources in determining the outcome of the conflict. Also bring into the equation such factors as leadership, tactics and strategy, the co-operation of allies and fighting ability.

Question 3 might draw you into an exhaustive narrative account of the course of the war. Step back from this and give an analytical explanation of the main features of the war (leadership, technology, resources, tactics and strategy and the strength of alliances, etc.) to demonstrate the part they played in the Allies' victory. Remember the same question could be presented as 'Why did the Axis powers lose the Second World War?'

Also attempt the following questions:

4. Why was there a greater loss of life in the Second World War compared with World War One?

5. Why did it take so long to defeat the Axis powers?

7 Into the Future: Post-1945 Developments and Conclusion

POINTS TO CONSIDER

The following chapter provides a survey of the major features of war from 1945 to 2000 with pointers to future developments. It concentrates on technological innovations and their impact upon strategy and the funding of warfare and defence. The chapter also seeks to offer conclusions on the characteristics of war over the last 300 years and their changing role in the nature of warfare.

1 Introduction

KEY ISSUE What have been some of the most striking changes in the nature of warfare over the last 300 years?

The main body of our study has taken us from the dynastic wars of the eighteenth century to the total wars of the twentieth century. This has led us from the smooth-bore musket to the atomic bomb, and from armies of 70,000 to forces of tens of millions. Of course military evolution does not come to a halt in 1945; developments set in train by World War Two continue at an alarming pace. The most visible of these has been the rate of change in military technology. 'Since 1945 weapon technology has expanded at a rate many times faster than that of all previous centuries put together'.[1] The implications of this for the planning of strategy and the very structure of military forces are still unfolding. The following sections examine the most significant areas of change and set them in the context of developments in the nature of warfare over the last three centuries.

2 Technology

KEY ISSUE What are the major developments in military technology during this period?

The last acts of World War Two, the destruction of two Japanese cities by atomic bombs, appeared to be a stark demonstration of the importance of military technology in modern war. Within months of the end of the war mutual suspicion and ideological antagonism shattered the victorious Grand Alliance leading to a bitter 'Cold War' and a sustained arms race unprecedented in peacetime. The two superpowers (USSR and USA) that emerged from the war became the leaders of powerful military and political alliances. The primary focus of the arms race between them was atomic weapons. By 1949 Russia had also developed the bomb, and it seemed that ideological antagonism might escalate into nuclear confrontation. The race now concentrated on increasing the numbers and the power of nuclear weapons, and the sophistication and range of their delivery systems. Following the development of the hydrogen (or fusion) bomb in 1953, the explosive power of weapons expanded year by year until it reached a peak in 1961 when the USSR exploded a device with the power of 4,000 Hiroshima-type bombs. This single weapon was more powerful than all the bombs dropped on Germany during the course of the Second World War. Scientists could devise even more powerful weapons, though this seemed futile as, in Churchill's words, 'they would only make the rubble bounce'.[2]

As well as the increase in the power of bombs there was a massive expansion in their number. By the late 1950s there were several thousand, by the late 1960s over 10,000, and by the mid-1980s 30,000. Military observers and satirists alike speculated on how many times over the world's population could be destroyed. One of the early constraints on the potential use of nuclear weapons was their delivery onto the target, as they were so large and heavy that they needed specially adapted heavy bombers. But in the mid-1950s more compact bombs and a more sophisticated, miniaturised in-built guidance system enabled them to be launched as missiles from jet planes, submarines, artillery or motor vehicles. The missiles increased in range so that Inter Continental Ballistic Missiles (ICBMs), with multiple warheads, could be fired from one side of the planet to the other to fall within hundreds of yards of their target. For Hew Strachan, 'The harnessing of explosive power to an effective delivery vehicle had transformed war more fundamentally than had the atomic bomb itself.'[3]

The increased competition and hostility of the Cold War ensured ever-greater funding of research and development of military technology. Conventional weapons, such as aircraft carriers, became larger and the improved version of the tank multiplied its power and speed. The jet fighter/bomber, introduced in 1950, was capable of twice the speed of its World War Two predecessors. Another post-war development, the helicopter, added greater flexibility to air-borne operations with their capacity for reconnaissance, troop transport and ground attack with machine gun and missiles.

From the late 1960s the terms 'electronic war' and 'computer war' were used to describe conflicts using electronically guided missiles and electronically enhanced weapons. With the greater speed and range of missiles and planes only computers could locate and track targets. By the 1980s all missiles, large or small, contained microprocessors; aircraft and ships would contain hundreds. Precision

Atomic test explosion over Bikini, 1946.

guided missiles (the most famous the cruise missile) used lasers, computers linked to satellite positioning systems and gun cameras to achieve pinpoint accuracy. They could be launched from air, land or sea hundreds of miles away to locate their programmed target, even sending back images of their progress and final destination. As Michael Ignatieff put it, war can now be conducted by remote control via images on a computer screen; we have entered an era of 'virtual war'.[4]

3 Strategy

> **KEY ISSUE** How has strategy attempted to deal with the new military technology and its limitations?

With the development of such an awesome range of weapons it seemed as if the nature of warfare was to be dictated by the most advanced destructive technology available. Yet due to the sheer destructive power of nuclear weapons this did not take place. Once both superpowers had nuclear weapons and the means to deliver them onto enemy cities a doomsday strategy was developed in which both sides made it clear that an attack on themselves, or their major allies, would lead to 'massive retaliation'. This was the policy with the appropriate acronym MAD (Mutually Assured Destruction). Therefore a nuclear attack by one superpower on the other would lead to a devastating escalation of the conflict with the result that for both sides victory would be indistinguishable from defeat and could even lead to the extinction of life on earth. This was the ultimate deterrent; nuclear war was to be avoided by the realisation of its potential horrors. Nuclear weapons therefore represent an ironic twist in the evolution of strategy, their greatest value lying not in their use, but in the threat of their use, no matter how unlikely the possibility.

Despite this practical constraint on the use of nuclear weapons it has not prevented their development by many other countries. Britain developed the bomb by 1953, France followed in 1960, in turn to be followed by China, Israel, India and Pakistan. At present up to 20 countries are believed to have the capacity to produce nuclear weapons. Yet the fact remains that in the half century since the end of World War Two no further nuclear weapons were used in spite of the heightened tensions of the Cold War. Nuclear weapons produced a 'Balance of Terror' that has so far helped prevent their use. However, even these most powerful of weapons have not prevented war at a 'sub-atomic' level. Since 1945 over 100 wars have occurred, many of them involving the nuclear powers but not their nuclear weapons. Indeed it is claimed that the possession of a nuclear arsenal has a moderating effect, as countries appear more secure and less trigger-happy. Countries such as China, India, Pakistan and Israel have been involved in far fewer wars since their adoption of nuclear weapons than they were before they joined the 'nuclear club'.

If the reluctance to engage in nuclear war for fear of the consequences demonstrated the limitations of technology in strategic planning then this was to be confirmed by the conduct of war below the level of both nuclear and conventional war. As many as three-quarters of all wars since 1945 have been 'sub-conventional' or guerrilla wars in which resistance, liberation or terrorist groups have taken against, and mostly defeated, technologically superior opponents. In the two decades following 1945 there were numerous successful wars of liberation by Asian and African militias against their European colonial masters.

In the 1960s and 1970s under the pressure of Cold War rivalry the two mighty superpowers found themselves drawn into struggles against guerrilla movements in third world countries, namely Vietnam and Afghanistan. It led to humiliating defeat for both. The most advanced military hardware – supersonic fighter-bombers, heavy tanks and artillery – were ineffective or irrelevant in the jungles of Vietnam or the mountains of Afghanistan. It was as much a failure of military doctrine and training as it was of technology. The superpowers, despite their massive material superiority, were ill equipped to deal with an enemy that did not conform to the established principles of conventional warfare. They faced an enemy with few modern weapons and without a conventional army that could not be distinguished from the surrounding population. The resistance movements were fired by an ideological intensity that was clearly absent in their opponents. Their commitment inspired greater levels of effort and the endurance of enormous losses to achieve their goals. Defeat in Vietnam and Afghanistan was so costly and humiliating for the superpowers that that they were both forced to reassess their strategic approach to military intervention.

After Vietnam the US treated military intervention with extreme caution, restricting themselves to strictly limited actions with fixed goals and preferably conducted by air power alone. Above all, losses to ground forces had to be minimised or totally eliminated. For America the solution was to be delivered by precision guided missiles, notably the 'Tomahawk' cruise missile. Previously attacks from the air were indiscriminate due to their inaccuracy. Bombing raids such as those of the Second World War, or even the Vietnam War, are now considered morally unacceptable and their effectiveness has been questioned. Precision guided bombs and missiles held out the hope of rapid victory achieved entirely from the air without the need to commit ground forces. The aim of war in the computer age is to 'blind the enemy' by striking at the nerve centres of their war effort: their command posts, computer networks and detection systems. Following this, if further action is necessary, air strikes and blockade could disable the enemy economy. Enemy ground forces, lacking co-ordination and air cover, could be smashed from the skies, such as in the devastating so-called 'turkey shoot' which destroyed the retreating Iraqi army on the Basra road in 1991. This new shape of warfare was further refined in the US-led coalition air-borne attack on Serbia in the Kosovo conflict of 1999. In this war 35 per cent of all bombs and missiles launched were precision guided, in the Gulf War of 1991 the figure was 8 per cent.

4 Resources and the Cost of War

> **KEY ISSUE** What impact did the cost of war and the arms race have on the major powers during this period?

A perennial constraint on the conduct of war has been the sheer cost of the undertaking. In the late twentieth century, under the pressure of the Cold War, it was not just the cost of war as much as the huge consumption of resources in being prepared for instant military response and the need to match the technological advances of one's opponent. In an age of rapid technological change and weapons obsolescence only the wealthiest powers could attempt to compete in the arms race. Even then there was a real danger of bankruptcy and collapse as the Soviet Union found to its cost in 1989. The US, the wealthiest country the world has ever seen, was driven into massive debt for many years by the cost of the Vietnam War. The cost of high-tech weapons was mind-boggling. A single cruise missile costs nearly half a million pounds, aircraft cost tens of millions and the most advanced radar-avoiding stealth bombers cost £1.5 billion pounds each. Their research and development costs dwarf even these figures.

As in previous ages the crippling cost of war and the preparation for war was used as a strategy itself. By the 1980s the Americans realised that the inefficient Soviet economy could not keep pace, economically or technically, with the next generation of computer warfare. The Americans deliberately stepped up their military spending and announced a programme, the Strategic Defence Initiative, to develop a defensive system against a nuclear attack. This projected system, dubbed 'Star Wars', was technologically unachievable. However, it was a significant factor in persuading the new Soviet leader, Mikhail Gorbachev, to end an arms race in which his country could no longer compete. As a result, from the late 1980s, the superpowers reached a number of agreements to dismantle many of the missiles targeted at each other and to reduce the number of warheads to 1950s levels. Yet the Soviet attempt to remove the economic burden of the arms race came too late to save it and its ideological empire from disintegration. The Cold War was over, decided not in battle but in the cost of competition.

5 Conclusion: 300 Years of Warfare

KEY ISSUE What has been the influence of cost and resources on warfare?

a) The Economic Constraint on Warfare

After having traced the changing nature of warfare over the last three centuries, we are now in a position to reflect on the degree of change and continuity over that time. The previous section, on the cost of war in the modern age, is a graphic illustration of the continuing import-ance of this particular feature of warfare. Eighteenth-century com-manders were extremely conscious of the ruinous expense of replacing and training troops. As a result they developed the tactics of manoeuvre rather than direct battle to exhaust the finances and sup-plies of enemy forces. During the quarter century of the French wars the economic war between Britain and Napoleon led to blockade and counter blockade. Resistance to Napoleon's Continental System and his ruthless exploitation of the conquered territories played a crucial part in his overthrow. The blockade of Germany in the First World War was an even more intense form of economic warfare leading to the deaths of 750,000 German civilians. The mobilisation of economies and the competition between them was a central feature of total war. The industrial wars of the twentieth century required the conversion of civilian economies into war economies and the maximisation of resources to outproduce the enemy. Finally the collapse of the Soviet bloc under the economic strain of Cold War competition is something the eighteenth-century commander would be proud of – the crushing of an opponent without having to meet in battle.

b) Technology, Tactics and Strategy

> **KEY ISSUE** How has the relationship between technology, tactics and strategy evolved over the last three centuries?

In our period of study, technology has played a major role in the conduct of warfare. The prevailing state of weapons development and transport, communications and detection technology are the main determinants of the tactics and strategy of war. In the first 100 years of our study the pace of weapons development appears virtually stationary by today's standards. By the nineteenth century the increased pace of technological development ushered in by the industrial revolution transformed the nature of warfare. War was revolutionised in its reach and scale by railways and the steam boat. Innovations in communications such as the telegraph, radio and the telephone transformed the co-ordination and control of military operations over vast distances. Mass produced modern weapons greatly expanded the casualties of war. By 1945 the development of the ultimate weapon of mass destruction, the atomic bomb, appears to have led military forces into a technological cul-de-sac. A weapon has been developed and taken up that is so powerful, and its consequences so unthinkable, that it dare not be used. Again there are echoes of eighteenth-century warfare: for the most advanced military powers all conflict must now be limited war.

The primary instrument of limited war in the modern age is the precision guided missile. This technology has the potential to revolutionise warfare. For the most advanced countries it offers the prospect of remote control war with few casualties to one's own forces. The technology can be applied to miniaturised, low intensity nuclear weapons and even, theoretically, to small arms fire. If attacks can be launched from thousands of miles away it places a huge question mark over the need for large army units, bomber aircraft or even aircraft carriers. Since the introduction of rifles and long range artillery the conflict zone has expanded and military observers have referred to 'the empty battlefield'. The cruise missile, aimed at an enemy's command and communication systems and his economic resources, has the potential to make the concept of the battlefield redundant.

c) War and the Civilian

> **KEY ISSUE** How has the relationship between the civilian and the armed forces changed over the last 300 years?

Central to the history of warfare over the last three centuries is the evolving relationship of modern societies and their armed forces. In the eighteenth century after the horrors of unlimited warfare in the Thirty Years War there was a deliberate attempt to isolate the impact of war from the civilian population. This was to be achieved through limited war aims, guaranteed supplies reducing the need for pillage, and the quartering of the armed forces away from the host population. There was little identification between the people and the armed forces. Armies were generally small and the troops were drawn from the least desirable and useful members of society. These armies fought not for the nation but for the king. The mass French Revolutionary Army of the *levée en masse* transformed war from a contest between kings into a struggle between peoples. This required the mobilisation of the population for military, economic and ideological purposes. Armies now went to war for their nation and its values; the civilian population supported them materially and increasingly identified with their cause and their fate.

These trends were reinforced by the impact of industrialisation on armies. The revolution in transport allowed bigger armies and required a greater contribution from the civilian population in terms of military service and resources. The total wars of the twentieth century were the high point of mass mobilisation and the blurring of the distinction between the roles of soldier and civilian. Since then the absence of wars between the most advanced states in the nuclear age has slowly eroded the close association between the civilian population and its armed forces. Military operations and costs are viewed with caution and even suspicion. With prolonged peace and the development of weapons that do not require mass forces, or a total war effort, mass mobilisation is considered redundant in the developed world. As a result the major powers have ended a two hundred year history of conscription and scaled down their forces to small, intensively trained and technically sophisticated specialists. The US armed forces, for example, has shed 36 per cent of their personnel since 1989, and defence spending has fallen from 6 per cent to 3 per cent of their gross domestic product.

d) Public Opinion

> **KEY ISSUE** How has public opinion had an increasing impact on the conduct of war in this period?

Running parallel with the evolving relationship between society and its armed forces is the increasing influence of public opinion on military affairs. In the age of authoritarian dynastic rule the notion of public opinion was non-existent in any form that we would recognise today. The host population regarded armies, often seen as alien and exploitative, with suspicion. The defence of the French Revolution required a mass army and a total war effort; to achieve both, ideological commitment had to be created and harnessed. To meet the challenge the remaining dynastic states had to respond in kind. Slowly, and often reluctantly, the dynastic armies evolved into forces of national defence.

The relationship and identification between people and their armed forces was further intensified by the modernising influence of industrialisation. Urbanisation and the increase in literacy rates and the popular press in the wake of mass education created a shared national consciousness. Public opinion strongly identified with the national cause and the armed forces. The expansion of the franchise provided an influential outlet to nationalist and militarist sentiment which played its part in the outbreak of the First World War. The total war effort of the two world wars required the mobilisation of entire populations and the manipulation of opinion to ensure support and unity. This was not difficult to achieve as these wars were seen as struggles for national survival and inspired great sacrifices for the war effort and intense hatred of the enemy. In the post 1945 period the likelihood of a major war seems a remote possibility to the populations of the Western world. When war is no longer associated with national survival it cannot count on public support.

This was most famously demonstrated during the Vietnam War, the first of the television wars. As the war dragged on under the intense scrutiny of the nightly news reports Americans witnessed the grisly realities of war brought direct to their living rooms. This was no longer the carefully scripted, upbeat message of World War Two newsreels, it was the continuous uncensored broadcast of the world's media. The Vietnam War was the most public war in history, and the American public did not like what they saw. From this point onwards, for democratic countries, the preparation of public opinion, at both a domestic and international level, was an essential pre-requisite for any military operation. This was seen in the American-led coalition attacks on Iraq in 1991 and Serbia in 1999. In these 'media wars' nightly briefings were given to justify the day's actions and to rebut the charges of brutality made by the enemy.

At the beginning of our study public opinion and its impact on military affairs was negligible. By the early twentieth century the mobilisation of public opinion was necessary for the conduct of total war. By the end of the century it was essential for even the most short term operation.

References

1   B. Perrett, *The Changing Face of Battle* (Cassell, 2000), p. 296.
2   M. van Cheveld, 'Technology and War', p. 299 in C. Townshend (ed), *The Oxford Illustrated History of Modern War*, (Oxford, 1997).
3   H. Strachan, *European Armies and the Conduct of War* (Routledge, 1983), p. 190.
4   M. Ignatieff, *Virtual War* (Vintage, 2001), p. 161.

Answering essay questions on Chapter 7

Although this chapter provides only a survey of developments after 1945 you should be capable of answering questions on the major military issues of the period. Here are some examples:

1. How far has military technology determined the nature of warfare since 1945?
2. How far is it true to say that there was a revolution in military strategy in the post-1945 period?

The style of question 1 should be familiar to you by now. It is asking you to consider the significance of one of the features of warfare in relation to all other relevant features. This period demonstrates a bewildering increase in the rate of weapons innovation. Their power and sophistication may cause us to overestimate their significance relative to other factors. Often this power was not realised in battle: after all, no nuclear weapons have been used since 1945, and both superpowers have suffered painful defeats against technologically inferior opponents. Remember technologies create possibilities, their adoption and effective use is determined by a host of other factors such as cost, political decisions, military conservatism and public opinion.

Question 2 asks you for an assessment of the degree of change in strategy during this period. Explain both the changes and the continuities. Also be aware of the categories of war and the strategies they have given rise to. These categories of war are: nuclear war (or at least the threat of it), conventional war, and sub-conventional war, such as guerrilla war and civil wars. The vast majority of wars have fallen into the last category.

It is also worthwhile considering essay questions from across the period 1700–2000.

3. 'Commanders win battles, resources win wars'. How far do you agree with this statement? Illustrate your answer by reference to examples drawn from the period 1740 to 2000.
4. Explain the changing role of public opinion in the conduct of war from 1793 to the present day.

Question 1 asks for a relative assessment of two major features of war. Provide examples from across this time span to illustrate the contribution of both. There is a current tendency to assert that superior resources are the sole reason for victory in war; the defeat of Napoleon and the two world wars are usually offered as evidence for this. But there are a number of examples which argue against this assumption, such as the leadership of Frederick the Great in the Seven Years War, and the victories of Vietnam and Afghanistan against superpowers with far greater resources and advanced weapons.

Question 2 focuses on the growing importance of public opinion in the conduct of war. Note that the starting point is significant in that it is the first major mobilisation of public support to raise and equip a mass army, the *levée en masse*. Further examples can be taken from the Allies' response to the threat of Napoleon, the growth in the importance of public opinion due to the modernising effect of industrialisation, and the total wars of the twentieth century. Finally the late twentieth century with its constant media vigilance (at least in the developed world), has raised public opinion to new levels of influence on the conduct of war.

Further Reading

General

There are a number of general books on this subject which cover the specified period.

The best introduction still remains **M. Howard**, *War in European History* (Oxford, 1976). This brilliantly concise study traces warfare from the eighth century to the 1970s within the space of 150 pages. Also excellent, especially on tactics and strategy, is **H. Strachan**, *European Armies and the Conduct of War* (Routledge, 1983). **L. Addington**, *The Patterns of War since the Eighteenth Century* (Indiana University Press, 1984) is a very clear account and includes more on America's wars. **J.F.C. Fuller**, *The Conduct of War 1789–1961* (Da Capo Press, 1992), is a highly readable if polemical account from one of Britain's most famous soldier-historians.

For the relationship between war and society see the '*War and European Society*' series, especially **G. Best**, *War and Society in Revolutionary Europe 1770–1870* (Sutton, 1998) and **B. Bond**, *War and Society in Europe 1870–1970* (Sutton, 1998).

Specific Wars or Periods

a) Dynastic Warfare has not produced a huge volume of books, but very useful is **J. Black**, *European Warfare 1660–1815* (Routledge, 1994) and, by the same author, *A Military Revolution* (Macmillan, 1991). For a concentration on Frederick the Great, see **D. Showalter**, *The Wars of Frederick the Great* (Longman, 1996). Also see **M.S. Anderson**, *War and Society of the Old Regime 1618–1789*.

b) The Napoleonic Wars, and especially Napoleon himself, have inspired a vast number of books, the Revolutionary Wars less so. On the Revolutionary period see **T.C.W. Blanning**, *The French Revolutionary Wars 1787–1802* (Longman, 1996). For Napoleon the list is virtually endless but a standard is **G. Rothenberg**, *The Art of Warfare in the Age of Napoleon* (Spellmount, 1997, originally published in 1978). A very good modern study is **C.J. Esdaile**, *The Wars of Napoleon* (Longman, 1995).

c) War in the nineteenth century is dealt with well by **G. Wawro**, *Warfare and Society in Europe 1792–1914* (Routledge, 2000). Also see the appropriate sections in the previously mentioned *War and European Society* books by **G. Best** and **B. Bond**.

d) The First World War has produced a vast literature covering all imaginable aspects of the war. Recommended are **S.C. Tucker**, *The Great War* (UCL, 1998), **K. Robbins**, *The First World War* (Oxford, 1984) and **V. Brendon**, *The First World War* (Hodder and Stoughton, 2000). An excellent collection of essays by current leading authorities is **H. Stachan (ed.)**, *The Oxford Illustrated History of the First World War* (Oxford, 1998).

e) The Second World War has an even larger bibliography than the First World War. Especially recommended are **R. Overy**, *Why the Allies Won* (Pimlico, 1995), **R.A.C. Parker**, *The Second World War* (Oxford, 1989), **A.W. Purdue**, *The Second World War* (Macmillan, 1999) and **M. Kitchen**, *A World in Flames* (Longman, 1990).

f) Books on the post-1945 period have the disadvantage of becoming rapidly outdated as they are overtaken by further technological developments. However, the following are useful and interesting: **M. van Creveld**, *The Transformation of War* (The Free Press, 1991), **M. Kaldor**, *New and Old Wars* (Polity Press, 1998). An interesting polemic on modern war and the shape of future wars is **M. Ignatieff**, *Virtual War: Kosovo and Beyond* (Vintage, 2001).

Glossary

attrition The name given to the tactic adopted in the First World War to wear down the enemy by inflicting continuous heavy casualties e.g. Verdun.

Balance of Terror The precarious balance of power between rival nuclear powers. *Also see* MAD.

barracks Military base for lodging soldiers.

barrage A co-ordinated and sustained artillery attack.

blitzkrieg Lightning War. Co-ordinated, mobile warfare based upon the use of tanks, aircraft and motorised infantry. Mostly associated with early Nazi advances 1939–41.

blockade Naval action to prevent war materials, sometimes including food, from reaching the enemy.

breech Chamber at the back of a rifle or big gun into which the bullet or shell is placed.

canister Artillery shell of thin metal filled with musket balls or scrap that disintegrated as it left the cannon to spray the enemy with deadly fire.

column Attacking infantry formations favoured by the French revolutionaries and Napoleon. 50 to 80 men across the front and nine to 12 men deep to charge the enemy.

company Infantry grouping of approximately 100 men.

corps An army force of two or three divisions, approximately 30,000 men. An innovation of Napoleon and copied by all other armies.

cruise missile Precision-guided missile using lasers, computers and satellite positioning systems to navigate itself to a target.

depot A store of military equipment and supplies.

division An army force of two or more brigades, approximately 10,000 men.

doctrine The overarching concept of how a nation's forces will approach war.

dog-fight Individual battle between opposing fighter planes.

Final Solution The Nazi term for the attempt to wipe out Europe's Jewish population which resulted in the murder of six million Jews.

General Staff The highest command of the army responsible for planning and operations. The 'brain' of the army.

grenadiers Companies of bigger, stronger men used to make bayonet charges against the enemy. The shock troops of the eighteenth century.

guerrilla war War fought by irregular forces against regular armies.

Howitzer Short-barrelled artillery gun to fire heavy shells at a high angle of fire.

ICBM Inter Continental Ballistic Missile.

levée en masse The mass call to arms of the French people to defend the revolution in 1793.

Lewis Gun Portable light machine gun (26 pounds) of the British army.

limited war Warfare limited in its impact by moral, economic and physical constraints. Most closely associated with the eighteenth century.

logistics The procurement and delivery of all military supplies and personnel.

MAD Mutually Assured Destruction. Mutual threat by US and USSR that a nuclear attack against them would be met with massive nuclear retaliation.

magazine Ammunition container attached to a gun to pass the bullets into the breech for rapid firing. Also a building to store military supplies.

Maginot Line Heavy French defensive fortifications built along the Franco-German border in the early 1930s.

Maxim gun First fully automatic, belt-fed, water-cooled machine-gun, capable of firing 600 rounds a minute. Invented by Hiram Maxim.

militarism The civilian population's acceptance of military values and their identification with the armed forces.

mitrailleuse Early French version of the machine gun, hand-cranked.

mobilisation The final preparations for war; the calling up, equipping and delivery of an army ready for action. Also, in the modern age, the mobilisation of the civilian population and the economy for the war effort.

mortar Light artillery weapon with a high angle of fire.

musket Infantryman's weapon, in which bullet and propellant were loaded down the muzzle of the gun. In use until latter half of the nineteenth century. Forerunner of the rifle.

No-Man's-Land Fire-zone between enemy forces.

pike Long defensive thrusting spear used by infantrymen before the introduction of the bayonet.

platoon Tactical army grouping of approximately 30–40 men.

propaganda Presentation of news and information (often unreliable) calculated to boost morale at home and/or deflate the morale of the enemy.

radar Radio detection and ranging system to detect aircraft and other targets.

reconnaissance To gather information on enemy positions and strength. Initially carried out by the cavalry, taken over by the air force and electronic detection, radar, etc.

reserves Troops held back in reserve to be committed at the decisive moment to turn the battle.

rifle Hand-held infantry weapon fired from the shoulder. The inside of the barrel has long spiral grooves cut into it (rifling) to spin the bullet for greater accuracy and distance. Rifling has also been applied to larger artillery guns.

SDI Strategic Defence Initiative, projected US defensive shield against nuclear attack. Dubbed 'Star Wars' by the media.

shrapnel Fragments from exploding shells, grenades or bombs. Named after its inventor Lieutenant Henry Shrapnel in 1784.

skirmishers Light infantry used in advance of main body of eighteenth and nineteenth century forces to move and fire in flexible fashion.

storm troops Well-armed mobile soldiers trained to achieve rapid breakthrough.

strategic bombing Air raids against an enemy population aimed at the war economy and civilian morale.

strategy The setting of the higher aims and conduct of war.

tactical bombing The use of an air force in support of an army on the battlefield.

tactics The detailed methods and procedures by which strategic aims are achieved.

total war A war effort requiring the total mobilisation of the entire society and its resources.

Index